By Michael Cohen (U.S.A.), wheel-thrown "weed holders" painted with blue and gray glazes, approximately 10" high.

POTTERY
STEP - BY - STEP
By Henry Trevor

Watson-Guptill Publications
NEW YORK

Manufactured in the U. S. A.

ISBN 0-8230-4225-1

Library of Congress Catalog Card Number: 66-13000

First printing, 1966
Second printing, 1968
Third printing, 1971

TABLE OF CONTENTS

Slab-built vase with thrown foot, glazed, by John Tuska (U.S.A.).

Pottery is one of the oldest of all crafts. It was practiced many thousands of years ago by Egyptians on the banks of the Nile, and it is practiced today, in rather less primitive fashion, by studio potters all over the world, not to mention the great commercial potteries such as the giant Arabia factory in Finland. One of the reasons why pottery making has survived for so long is that it is a simple and functional craft which gives satisfaction to the maker and service to the purchaser. In addition, throughout the centuries, pottery has been shown to be truly a thing of beauty — by the Greeks, by the Romans, by the Tang and Sung Dynasty potters of China, by the Koreans, and, of course, by the American Indian.

Ours is an age of mass production, of standardization — of the conveyor belt. Perhaps this may be the reason for an interesting contrary trend toward arts and crafts, toward making things oneself. This trend is very much reflected in the art and trade schools, as well as in our high schools — and in recent years no craft has been more popular than pottery. Nearly all modern schools are now equipped with pottery departments, and there is great competition to partici-pate. This feeling for a sense of craft, for making things oneself, is very important. If we have actual physical contact with our materials we are the better able to understand them and appre-ciate their true purposes. Fortunately clay is hardly one of those materials which can be used for good or bad — its uses are highly beneficial to mankind, ranging from pots as things of beauty to kitchen utensils and onward to plumbing fixtures, electrical insulators, building brick, build-ing and drainage tile, etc.

Pottery making is, in fact, only one of several industries which revolve around the use of clay, but it has the advantage of being, and having always remained, an essentially individual craft. That is why today it is being taken up by more and more people, both as a challenge and a satisfaction. A fortunate result of this increased public interest is that it has enabled manu-facturers of equipment to bring down their prices to a level which can reasonably be considered by almost anyone. A couple of decades ago anyone wanting to start a pottery of his own at home would have needed substantial capital. This is no longer such a stumbling block. It is possible today to start a home pottery for no more than the capital outlay that would be required to become a movie photographer or a sailing enthusiast.

For this reason there must be today many students of pottery who would like to develop their talent by setting up a pottery of their own, and the aim of this book is to provide first a grounding in the basic essentials of pottery making, and also to provide necessary information about how and where to purchase equipment, and also how to go about the business of actually starting a small pottery.

Because pottery making is essentially a handcraft, it does not demand an inordinate amount of equipment. First in importance is *clay*, the potter's raw material, and therefore the second chapter of this book introduces you to clay and its properties. With clay alone you can make pots, just as the primitive natives did, using your fingers as modeling tools; or you can produce a much wider and more ambitious range of pottery by using a potter's wheel. History records that there were potter's wheels in existence more than four thousand years ago, and in its basic principle the wheel has not greatly changed through the centuries. The primary need is to have a wheel rotating at considerable speed, sufficient for a lump of clay to be changed into a cylindrical shape by a combination of that speed and the centrifugal force, and pressure from the potter's hands. In early years the wheels had notches along the edges and were pushed round with a stick; later this was varied into the kick wheel, used in many potteries today. A kick wheel has a small wheel head at the top of a rod joined at the bottom to a heavier wheel, which in turn is operated by a shaft which the potter kicks. Since the object of the kicking is merely to supply motive force to make the wheel head turn, it has been a logical step, making use of modern methods, for electrically operated wheels to have been developed, which enable the potter to give all his attention to the throwing. Your choice of wheel may depend on circumstance and economics; there is, in any case, no harm in beginning with a kick wheel, which you can purchase fairly cheaply or, if you are handy with tools, make yourself (you çan obtain a complete set of plans, with suggestions as to sources for materials, for about $3.50 from the Potter's Wheel Design Co., P.O. Box 29153, Los Angeles, California). But later on you will probably find an electric wheel more convenient.

Apart from a wheel the only other essential piece of a potter's equipment is a kiln. Kilns vary considerably in size, and you will find fuller details about them in the chapter on equipping a pottery of your own. Perhaps I should mention here that you can build an electric kiln of your own — on the other hand, there is a wide selection of ready-made kilns now on the market. For the purposes of this book I am assuming that you would choose to use electrically operated kilns, since they are simple and reasonably economical to operate, but you should be aware that there are also kilns which operate on gas, oil, wood, and sometimes a combination of one or more fuels. The sort of kiln which the earliest people used was a fairly crude affair of dried mud fired by burning wood. This would be reasonably effective, and you could experiment if you have a large garden. The fact that most modern potters have turned to more scientific methods is merely because they are more convenient, and quicker. It is indeed one of the delights of pottery that both beginner and professional can obtain pleasure from its practice.

The aim of this book is not to turn you into a professional potter — it is, rather, to prepare you for becoming one if you should decide you want to be. As I write this book I am imagining a typical reader to be someone who has always been rather drawn to ceramics, perhaps has some artistic leanings in general, but has never even got so far as to attend classes. So I shall assume that you have no real technical knowledge of pottery and how to make it, and my aim will be to introduce you to the subject, explain its processes, to instruct you in the

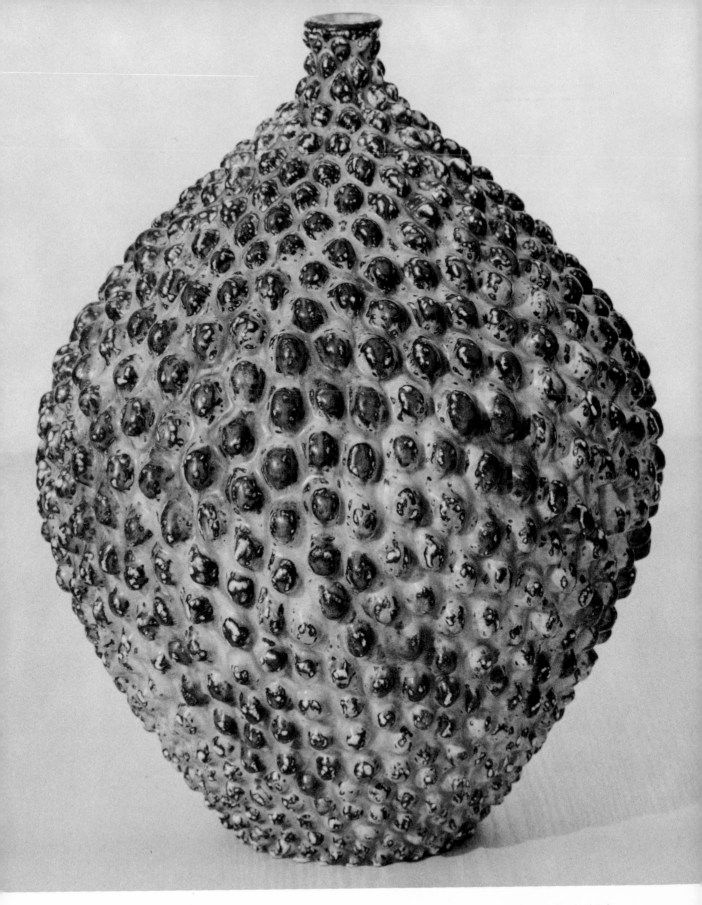

Glazed stoneware by the Danish ceramist Axel Salto.

various methods of throwing, decorating, glazing, and so on, and finally to provide as much information as you would need to set up a home pottery and carry on from there. At the end of this book you will find a list of some reading matter and other relevant details which may help you in your quest. Any unfamiliar terms are defined in the glossary.

Clay is the basic material of pottery, and just as the craft itself is a very ancient one, so the material originally derives from many centuries past — for it derives, really, from decomposed granite rock. Clay is to be found in most parts of the country, particularly around river beds, but in certain areas it is more common — New York, for instance, and Pennsylvania and Ohio. It is quite an interesting experiment to investigate the clay position in your own area, if only as a piece of geological detective work. At one time I lived in a large country house where a clay bed ran under the garden, and it was possible to go out and dig up thick chunks of yellow clay. Needless to say this was by no means the pure finished clay, such as you would use in the studio or at a pottery class. Raw clay dug from the ground would be full of impurities, and before it could be used these would have to be removed by spreading the clay out to dry in the sun and then washing it by mixing with water, and sieving. These processes are so laborious that they are not generally to be recommended except, as I have said, as an experiment.

Such cleansing processes are, of course, applied by the large clay manufacturers in reducing raw clay to the "prepared" state, ready for use by potters. It would be well worth your while some time to arrange a visit to a commercial clay operation. Here the raw clay is mixed and sieved and passed into tanks where mechanical agitation is used for stirring. Finally the liquid clay is pumped into large filter presses and then forced through fine-mesh cloths. After the surplus water is removed there is left a series of thin sheets of plastic clay, which in turn are kneaded and wedged to the right consistency.

Earthenware

In general there are three types of clay — earthenware, stoneware, and porcelain. Earthenware is usually made from a natural clay, and its firing temperature (i.e. the temperature at which the glaze fuses) is below 2000° F. If earthenware were fired at any greater temperature, it would lose its shape. Being comparatively soft in consistency, earthenware is porous, unless covered by a glaze. It is usually red or buff in color, often quite dark.

Stoneware

Stoneware fires at a much higher temperature, above 2300° F. It is much stronger than earthenware and nonporous, so that even unglazed such pots will hold water. Its higher firing temperature means that the color effects of glazes are more limited, though often more subtle.

Four works by U.S. potter Toshiko Takaezu, all thrown, with brushed decoration over thick white glaze.

By Dorothy Midanik of Canada, small slab-built boxes with over-all iron oxide and white glaze circles on the lids.

Porcelain

Porcelain is stronger still, and fires at an even higher temperature — from 2300° to 2670° F. (when the clay body and the glaze fuse together and achieve a translucent effect).

A word should also be said about "chinaware," which is a somewhat different composition, being made up from kaolin, ball clay, flint, and feldspar. This is the material that is used a great deal by the large commercial potteries, where facilities are available for firing twice, or even three times — once at 2200° to 2280° F., then later at lower temperatures to enable any decoration to be added.

In a book such as this it is not possible to go into too much technical detail, and if you wish to analyze clay further I would advise you to read some of the books listed in the Bibliography. The main point you need to grasp is that earthenware, the sort of clay you are most likely to use, is a plastic, pliable material, which can be pushed or pinched or molded or pressed or thrown into all kinds of shapes; that these shapes when put in a kiln will harden at certain specific temperatures; and that after these clay shapes have been covered with glazes, these will in turn fuse or melt at specific temperatures to provide a watertight, colorful coating or skin.

Clay, then, is a very important property. The first thing you should do is to get used to the feel of it. Pick up a lump and play around with it; try and see what strange shapes you can make. This, in fact, is how the earliest potters began, only in their case they had to learn by trial and error the sad fact that raw clay, containing impurities, would simply blow up when fired. You can reap the benefit of centuries of experience; the clay you use, as supplied by the established clay manufacturers, will be as pure as it can be, ready — almost — for immediate use.

Wedging

Notice my qualification. For though your clay is plastic and clean, it will still need a certain treatment which only the potter can apply — that is what is known as wedging. This is simply a way of ensuring that all traces of air are removed from the clay to be used. The usual procedure is to take a large slab of clay and — using a strong surface, such as a kitchen table, as a base — cut the slab into two halves with a fine wire, lift one high up in the air and bang it down upon the other half. Then repeat the process again and again, banging two halves together, turning them over, cutting off another half, banging it down, and so on. It's hard physical work, but necessary; usually about ten minutes of wedging is sufficient. A variety of the wedging process is kneading, rather as used with baker's dough, turning the lump over and over and pressing down into the center with the palm of your hand.

When the clay can be cut through at any point without showing air bubbles it is ready for use. Your clay is now thoroughly wedged, and generally the potter would next divide it into separate balls of clay in preparation for throwing a series of pots. Before, however, we reach this important stage of pottery making, let us first consider some of the ways of making pots without using a wheel.

WEDGING CLAY

1. Wedging is a process which removes all traces of air from the clay. To begin, take a slab of clay and cut it in two halves with fine wire.

2. The air bubbles can be readily seen.

3. Now, lift one half high in the air, bang it down on the other half, firmly knead the clay, and repeat the process again and again for at least ten minutes.

4. When the clay is thoroughly wedged, it can be cut through at any point without showing air bubbles.

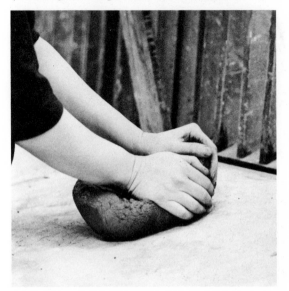

Thrown teapot by Fred Bauer (U.S.A.), with brushed decoration over clear glaze, 9″ high.

Raku pot by Paul Soldner (U.S.A.). Form was thrown, then paddled to achieve the final shape.

Covered stoneware jar by Fred Bauer (U.S.A.), wheel-thrown, with brown glaze and incising.

When you take a lump of clay in your hand, what is your almost instinctive reaction? I think it is very likely to be this—your fingers begin playing with the clay, moving it round and round, squeezing and poking it into odd shapes—in fact, pinching the clay.

The Pinch Method

Pinchware is a name given to one of the earliest and indeed most obvious forms of making pots. An obvious application of this technique would be in the making of figures, but in fact it is possible to use the pinchware method to make small, rather crude pots—and indeed this is how natives used to make them.

In brief this is what you do. Take a lump of clay, roll it into a ball, rest the ball in one hand, and then press your thumb into the center of the ball while working it round and round in the palm of your hand. Carry on with this process until you have hollowed out a small container. Naturally the scope of pinchware, as far as actual pots are concerned, is rather limited, but using this method you can make bowls, ash trays, and small dishes, as well as flower vases. While the result is bound to be fairly crude, you can reduce this effect by occasionally moistening your thumb and fingers and continually smoothing over any rough edges.

Coiling

Coiling is the name we give to one of the earliest of all forms of pottery making. The reason for this method going back so far is very simple: it was, originally, the apparent way to make pots. It is popularly supposed that our ancestors came to pottery from basket making, and to them it seemed quite logical to apply the same technique of building up a shape in coils.

To make a coiled pot, you must first roll out lengths of clay in strips of about half an inch. in diameter and, say, a foot or eighteen inches in length. When you have several of these lengths ready, you can start building up your pot, starting with the base. Begin at the center winding your coiled lengths round and round. As you go along, remember to moisten the fingers of your free hand and continually smooth over the coiled surface so that the base becomes smooth and without cracks.

When you have completed using one coiled length, simply join on the next—a good tip here is to make a slice in the end of each coil so that it can be fused or joined properly. Keep on coiling until the base is of the required width. Next comes the building up of the sides. The procedure is much the same, except that now you will be coiling vertically instead of horizontally. This means that while coiling with one hand you will need to use gentle pressure from the fingers of the other hand from the inside to help the wall to coil upwards. When one coil is ended, join another as before. Continue coiling until your wall is as high as you want, being careful always to keep the wall steady and also to smooth any cracks or gaps. If your pot is to be of any sort of height, then of course the wall would tend to sag after a certain stage. The best thing here is to stop work after reaching three inches in height and wait for the bottom clay to dry off, resuming coiling when this has occurred. Above a height of six inches, the clay used for a coiled pot requires the addition of feldspar at the wedging stage to give it sufficient strength to withstand disintegration during firing. Continue until your pot is made to your requirements, always remembering your smoothing processes (the outside of the pot, by the way, does not have to be smoothed, and many potters prefer to leave the coiled outline as a part of the general decorative effect).

Within reason, coiling can be used to make all kinds of pots — and some of the most striking effects, of course, have been obtained with huge pots which would have been beyond the power of a thrower. Also, asymmetrical shapes, unless the potter distorts wheel pieces, can only be made by coiling or slab methods.

Coiling can offer much pleasure and is always of use for initiating people into pottery making; children, in particular, seem to find this process attractive.

Molds

Mold making is used on a large scale in commercial potteries, but frankly it does not have a great appeal to the studio potter for in essence it is a factory process. If you make a pot with your hands, that is an individual and, in its way, unique creation. If you make a pot in a plaster mold (the type usually used) then all you are doing is producing a standardized article, as is done in thousands of factories. There is the one advantage of a mold to a small potter, however. It does enable him to make pots of unusual shapes, which could not be produced on the wheel.

The Slab

Slab pottery is a simple method of rolling out sheets of clay and then pressing or cutting them into specific shapes. You can use several slabs of flat clay, alone or in combination with coiling, to make a variety of vertical forms or flat trays without using a mold or the wheel. The process is a simple and obvious one; you merely cut out the required number of sides (base, walls, top, etc.) and then weld them together with your wetted fingers. A modeling tool can be used to cut away the inside of a lid or to make any other required apertures or cutaways.

Small covered jar by U.S. potter Patricia Bauer, with thick brown and black glazes.

A thrown bowl by Gertrud and Otto Natzler (U.S.A.) with "crater" glaze in gray, sand, and blue.

Simple jewelry can be cut from a clay slab, including beads for stringing, earrings, buttons, etc. Most attractive earrings can be made by using a sharp knife or modeling tool to cut out various shapes—circular, hexagonal, diamond, or leaf-shaped, and so on. Later these can be decorated and glazed (remember to glaze on the front only so that the earring can be fired without sticking to the floor of the kiln) and finally fitted with the usual earclasps which are fixed on with glue. A method by which you can glaze earrings on both sides is the same as that used for glazing beads: make a small hole at the top of each earring and then thread it on a length of old element wire and hang it across the inside of the kiln on two supports; this way there is no danger of sticking. Subsequently these holed earrings can be fitted to earclasps by hooks which fit into the small holes.

Beads offer plenty of scope for originality of glazing and decoration. To make them, cut your slab into strips and then cut these into regular sections; roll each one into a neat small ball which in turn you pierce with a length of wire. Then slip and glaze and thread on a length of element wire. When the beads are fired, string them on lengths of leather such as used for shoelaces.

THE PINCH METHOD

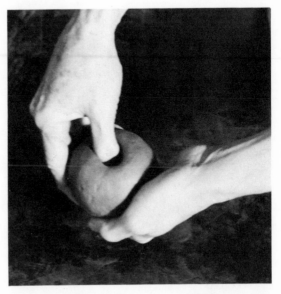

1. To make a pot by the pinch method, take a lump of clay and roll it into a ball.

2. Press your thumb into the center while working the ball of clay round and round in the palm of your hand.

4. Although the final shape is somewhat crude, it can be smoothed out by moistening your thumb and fingers and smoothing over any rough spots.

3. Continue this process until you have hollowed out a small container.

COILING

1. To build a coiled pot, first take a lump of clay and roll it into a small length.

2. Continue rolling until the clay becomes a long, narrow strip.

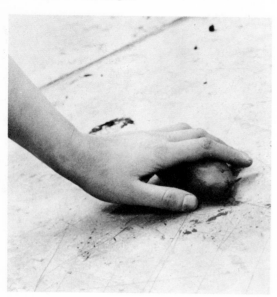

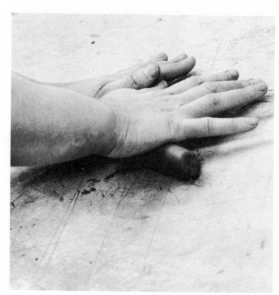

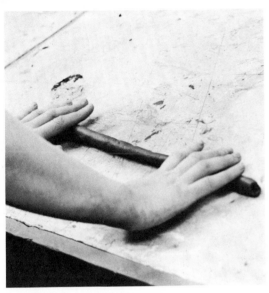

3. Coils for a small pot should be approximately one-half an inch in diameter and twelve to eighteen inches long—and you will need several of them.

4. Take one of the clay strips and start winding it around itself for the base of the pot.

5. Keep coiling until the base is the width you want.

6. As you go along, moisten your fingers and continually smooth over the coiled surface.

7.   To build up the sides, join a fresh strip of clay to the base and coil vertically, instead of horizontally.

9.   Always be careful to support the wall of the pot from the inside as you coil, to prevent it from sagging. Also remember to smooth the inside of the pot. You may prefer to leave this scalloped effect, rather than smooth out the sides.

8.   Joining other coils to the first ones, continue building until the sides of the pot are as high as you want.

THE SLAB

1. To make a slab—or thick sheet—of clay, you will need two flat boards of the same thickness and a wood rolling pin.

2. Roll out a ball of clay between the boards.

3. Work the clay until it is as even and regular as possible.

4. A modeling tool is used to cut the slab into the specific shapes needed for a slab pot.

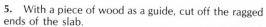
5. With a piece of wood as a guide, cut off the ragged ends of the slab.

6. Next, cut the required number of sides — base and walls — for your pot. Measure each slab to be sure they conform in size.

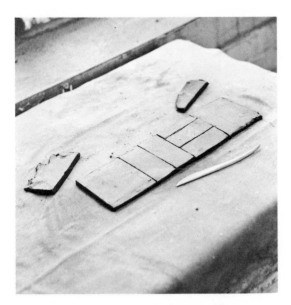

7. The clay slab cut and ready for assembly.

8. Score one edge of the base element with your modeling tool.

9. Score the attaching slab along its bottom edge.

10. Using the modeling tool, place some slip along the scored edge of the base piece.

11. Attach the two scored edges. The slip in the scored clay helps hold the sections together. Continue this process in building the rest of the pot.

12. Trim off any overlapping elements.

13. Smooth over the join at the base with the modeling tool.

14. In the same manner, smooth out the joins inside the pot.

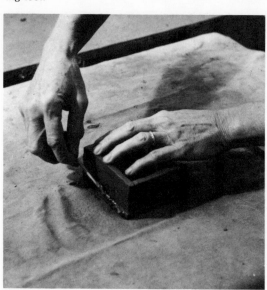

JEWELRY

1. To make a simple necklace of clay beads, roll several neat, small balls of clay.

3. Pierce the beads with a piece of wire, then thread them on length of cord or leather. If they are to be glazed, they should be threaded on a length of element wire.

2. Take some more clay and cut out several small rectangular shapes, roughly the size of the balls.

Raku vase by Charles Plosky (U.S.A.).

Once you have mastered the various methods of shaping clay by pinching, coiling, and molding, then it is likely you will feel better prepared for turning to the potter's main art, the art of *throwing*. So far you have been familiarizing yourself with clay and its properties, and you will have discovered something of its malleability and resilience. However, so far you have been dealing with clay as a comparatively dead thing. Now you are about to see clay come startlingly alive.

Things Required

The first important thing, if you are going to practice throwing pots, is to make quite sure that everything necessary is on hand. First things first — your *clay*. Take a lump off your supply of clay, and subject it to a thorough kneading and wedging to remove all air bubbles. Next you will need to prepare the clay for actual throwing by separating it into a series of portions, rolled up into balls. Place them in a row on a *board* or *shelf* at the side of the wheel, within easy reach of your hand. At the same time remember to place another board or fireclay shelf along the back of your wheel, or at the other side, to receive the finished pots.

What other accessories will you need? Well, you will have your own choice, but here are a few which I find useful — a *sponge* for absorbing water from the outside and inside of the pots; a *needle* or other sharp instrument for trimming the rims of the finished pots; a length of *chamois leather* for smoothing down the pots and lips, etc.; a length of *copper wire* (each end tied round a piece of wood to give a handle) for cutting pots away from the wheel — and of course a *bowl of water* into which periodically you can dip your fingers. Also, if you are intending to throw pots of the same or specified height, you will need some method of estimating the height — some potters fix a permanent *caliper* on the top of the wheel, or you can measure by ruler.

Centering the Pot

So we come to the actual act of throwing. Make yourself quite at ease and pick up a clay ball; throw it down hard on the center of your wheel, which you have set in motion.* As the ball spins round your first task will be to center it. After dipping your fingers in water, rest your elbows on the wheel box and clasp the ball of clay with both hands, pulling it towards the

*A note here about controlling the speed of your revolving wheel. With a kickwheel remember that to make the wheel go faster you need to kick more frequently, and conversely, to reduce speed slow down the rate of kicking. With an electric wheel, with probably two or three gears, begin in the low gear and increase your speed by switching to the middle or top gears.

A large planter by Nan Bangs McKinnell (U.S.A.) with ribbed handles and rim, applied decoration.

By William Wyman (U.S.A.), slab-built cookie jar with thrown lid, glazed in brown, gray, and blue, 13" high.

center of the wheel. This horizontal pressure will cause the clay to tend to rise in the center; you now put the base of your thumb on this cone and press it down again. Repeat this process continuously until the lump of clay has become smoothed out and revolves symmetrically. It is now centered.

Opening Out

The next stage is to open out your ball of clay. Put your right thumb firmly into the middle of the spinning ball and press downward; this will cause the clay to open outward. Now with your right fingers inside the aperture thus formed and your left hand supporting the outside wall, draw the clay outward to widen the base.

Drawing Up

When this is done your next step is to draw up the walls of the pot. This is done quite simply, keeping the wheel spinning at a regular rate, by putting the fingers of one hand inside the pot and hooding the outside wall with the fingers of your other hand, and then literally drawing the clay upward by pressure from the fingers inside the pot. Be certain they bring the clay up smoothly to ensure an even thickness—and let your hands rise with the clay. At intervals dip your fingers in water; this keeps the clay moist for easy manipulation. Continue the drawing up process until the pot has reached the required height.

If you were attempting to throw a very large pot then you might emulate the professional potters who take a large lump of clay, center it, raise it to the shape of a thick cylinder, and *then* open it out by pressing down the center with a clenched fist. This has the effect of making the walls rise up as the hand pushes down, and is a satisfactory alternative method of raising.

Shaping

Now comes the shaping of your pot; for instance, you may want to make the top portion curve first inward and then outward. This is done by a process known as *collaring*—that is, putting your fingers around the neck of the pot and squeezing gently (as perhaps one might attempt to choke someone). Alternatively, if you wish to make a pot bulge outward, put one hand inside, hold the fingers of the other on the outside for support, and literally push the wall outward, against the spinning movement.

Trimming

When your general shape has been created you should then trim the rim; this is done by picking up your needle and holding it about a quarter of an inch below the level of the rim (which will probably be uneven) and then pushing it against the revolving top; this will result in a layer being whipped off and will give a level rim. Now smooth this rim with the piece of chamois leather. Next pick up your sponge and insert it inside the pot to absorb any excess moisture, and at the same time smooth the inner walls.

Removing

Finally, with the wheel still revolving, pick up your length of copper wire, hold it tightly between your two hands, and draw firmly across the wheel head to cut away the bottom of the pot. You can now remove your pot from the wheel by drying your hands and placing the palms gently against each side and lifting upwards. Place it on a shelf.

Well, you have thrown your first pot. No doubt it will seem a crude and frail thing, but at the same time' it will be a cylindrical shape, created out of a lump of clay. This cylinder is the basis of most thrown pots, but of course its final shape can be varied a good deal by collaring or opening out. It is possible, for instance, to give a pot a fairly narrow base and then open out the top to make a pleasant flared vase. Or a pot can be made either small and stubby or tall and graceful.

Not all pots are cylindrical, however—saucers, shallow bowls, plates, ash trays and other comparatively flat shapes are simply centered, opened out in the usual way, and then left without being raised. Incidentally, shallow pots of this kind can be turned into triangular or square shaped pots if you wish, by simply pushing in the sides and flattening corners, after they have been removed from the wheel.

There are a few pots which have a closed top. To make this kind, you collar the top to the narrowest possible neck, and then using your fingers, press down gently to join the two walls— you make your holes later by puncturing the clay with a sharp point.

I hope in my anxiety to describe the process of throwing simply I haven't made it sound too simple. It isn't, as you will find out by laborious trial and error. But then again it isn't particularly complicated; it is just one of those things that only practice can bring to attainment. There is no better way of learning the art of throwing than practice, practice, and more practice. At first you may be downhearted, but if you persevere you will gradually acquire the necessary confidence, and at last you will begin to feel in control of the clay—instead of the clay being in control of you, as so often seems the case at first.

MAKING A BOWL

1. Make yourself at ease at the wheel and take a large piece of clay in both hands.

2. Set the wheel in motion and throw the ball of clay down hard on it. The clay must now be centered, so that it revolves symmetrically.

3. When the ball of clay has been centered, press your right—or both—thumbs down into the middle of the spinning ball.

4. This will make the clay open.

5. With your right fingers inside the aperture you have just formed, and your left hand supporting the clay wall, draw the clay out to widen the base.

6. Continue opening the clay.

7. Open the clay until the base is as wide as you desire.

8. The next step is to draw up the walls of the bowl. Put the fingers of one hand inside the pot, hood the outside wall with fingers of your other hand, and draw the clay upward.

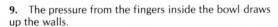

9. The pressure from the fingers inside the bowl draws up the walls.

10. Make sure that you bring the clay up smoothly to make the walls of the bowl of an even thickness.

11. By dipping your hands in water from time to time and keeping the clay moist, it will be easier to manipulate.

12. To shape the bowl, put one hand inside, place the fingers of the other on the outside for support, and push the wall outward against the spinning movement.

13. When the form of the bowl is completed, the rim should be smoothed down by pressing a chamois leather against the revolving edge.

14. The finished bowl, ready to be glazed and fired.

MAKING A POT

1. After your ball of clay has been thrown on the revolving wheel, it must be centered. To do this, wet your fingers and pull the clay toward the center of the wheel with both hands.

2. This horizontal pressure causes the clay to rise in the center.

4. Repeat this process until the lump of clay has smoothed out and is revolving symmetrically. The clay is now centered.

3. Place the bottom of your thumb on this cone and press it down again.

5. The next step is to open the clay. Press your thumbs firmly in the middle of the spinning ball and press down.

6. Now, place your right fingers inside the opening, and using your left hand as support on the outside wall, draw the clay out to widen the base.

7. The next step is drawing up. With fingers of one hand inside the pot, and fingers of the other hooding the outside wall, literally pull the clay up with pressure from the hand inside.

8. At intervals during the drawing up process, dip your fingers in water so that the clay will stay moist for easy manipulation.

9. If you bring the clay up smoothly—letting your hands rise with the clay—the walls of your pot will be of an even thickness.

10. Continue drawing up until the pot is the height you want.

11. At this point you will have a straight-sided cylinder revolving on the wheel.

12. You will now want to shape the pot. This can be done by placing one hand inside, using the other as support on the outside, and pushing the wall in or out as the pot revolves on the wheel.

13. Continue the shaping process.

14. Work and refine the form.

15. The pot is completed when you arrive at the shape you want.

TRIMMING THE RIM

1. The rims of most thrown pots are uneven, and you will probably want to trim them accurately. Raise the upper portion of the pot with your fingers.

2. Take a needle or other sharp pointed tool and hold it a quarter of an inch below the level of the rim.

3. By pushing the needle against the pot, a layer of clay will be whipped off, giving you a level rim.

4. Smooth the rim with a piece of chamois leather.

5. The finished pot.

TRIMMING THE BASE

1. To trim the base of a pot, the procedure is basically the same as for the rim. At an angle, hold a needle or other sharp tool against the base.

2. Push the instrument against the revolving pot.

3. A layer of clay will be whipped off in the process.

4. The angle of the trim can be adjusted by changing the angle of the trimming tool.

5. Remove the excess clay from around the base of the pot.

REMOVING THE POT

1. To remove the pot from the wheel, keep it revolving and take a length of copper wire between your hands.

2. Hold the wire taut and place it at the base of the far side of the pot.

3. Draw the wire firmly across the wheel head to cut away the bottom of the pot.

4. Dry your hands and place your palms gently against each side of the pot.

5. Lift up the pot.

6. Place the pot in a convenient place to dry.

Pottery making consists of a series of processes, and though some, like throwing, are obviously more important than others, all demand careful attention. For this reason you should pay special attention to what is known as the *handling* and *trimming* of pots, after they have been thrown.

Making a Lip

First, let us consider any further applications that may be necessary to the shaping of your pot. For instance, pitchers will require a lip. This is achieved very simply by a pulling action — you should support the mouth of the pot with the fingers of one hand, and use the first finger of your other hand to pull the edge of clay outward to form a lip. An alternative method of making a lip is to fashion it out of a separate piece of clay and then stick it on to the pot, but this is not generally favored as it is a weaker method.

Trimming

Another of the tidying up processes is known as trimming. First you should allow the pot to dry off for at least a day until the clay is leather hard. Then place the pot upside down on the wheel, pack wet clay around the sides to hold it firm, and, with the wheel spinning, use the sharp point of a trimming tool or knife to cut gently into the base of the pot, from the center outward. Continue this to cover about two thirds of the base area, leaving an outer rim. This trimming process is used principally for narrower pots, not for flat or shallow pots, which only need tidying up.

Handles

Many of your pots, such as cups and pitchers, will obviously need handles. These can be pulled from lumps of stiff clay, and if formed with plenty of water, take on the natural shape of the fingers. Handles are attached as soon as the piece is firm enough to work with. The join can be smoothed over, or you can leave finger marks as a natural decoration.

Lids

Certain pots may need lids, such as teapots. Usually lids are thrown on the wheel, rather as if you were throwing a small bowl, which is then turned upside down. First, center the clay and then with one finger or thumb make an opening in the middle and pull outward, forming a small wall. Then, using a trimming tool, cut away about a quarter of an inch from the outside, to make an outer rim. Naturally, you must remember first to measure the diameter of the pot into which your lid is to fit. Bear in mind that clay contracts when dried and bisque fired. (See Chapter 6.)

Spouts

If you throw a teapot, then you will need to make—separately—a teapot spout. First center a small ball of clay and then raise it up into a narrow cylinder, narrower at the top than at the bottom. You can use a sharp tool to poke down inside the cylinder and raise the narrow wall.

With your copper wire, remove the cylinder from the wheel, cut the thicker part of it across at an angle, and allow it to dry. Next select the point on your teapot where the spout is to be joined and make a series of small holes. Then stick the spout onto the side of the teapot, making sure to smooth over the join. You can, if you wish, pull a small lip on the end of the spout with your finger.

These are just a few of the handling and tidying up processes which should become an automatic part of your pottery making. Don't forget, too, to take a general look at your pots at that stage. After drying they may have one or two defects, perhaps a tiny lump of clay or an uneven surface; these should be smoothed out either with a knife or grinder. In the same way you should make quite sure that no foreign matter has become attached to your pots, as this might cause a blowout in the bisque firing. Sometimes it is quite a good idea to take a wet sponge and lightly sponge over the pots when they are semidry. (This is also done to them at a later stage, after they have been bisque fired and glazed to remove the glaze from the bottom so that they do not stick to the shelves.)

MAKING A PITCHER

1. First center the clay by pulling it toward the center of the wheel with both hands.

2. Be sure that your grip is firm.

3. The strong horizontal pressure will make the clay rise in the center.

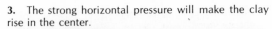

4. Place the base of your thumb on the cone.

5. Press the clay down again.

6. Repeat the centering process.

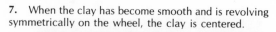

7. When the clay has become smooth and is revolving symmetrically on the wheel, the clay is centered.

8. Begin the opening process by pressing your thumb — or both thumbs — into the middle of the spinning ball.

9. With fingers of the right hand inside the newly formed aperture, and left hand on the outside wall, draw the clay outward to widen the base.

10. Now comes the drawing up stage of wheel throwing, with fingers of one hand inside the pitcher and the other hand on the outside as support.

11. The clay is brought up smoothly by applying pressure from the inside, and letting your hands rise with the clay.

12. Continue the drawing up process, keeping the clay moist for easy manipulation.

13. Soon your pitcher will be the height you want.

14. To shape your pitcher, give it a slight collar by putting your fingers around the neck of the pot and squeezing gently.

15. Further shape the pitcher by pushing the walls in or out against the spinning movement of the wheel.

16. Place one hand inside the pot and use the other on the outside for support.

17. The lower section of the pitcher can be made to bulge out in this same manner.

18. Refine the form continually.

19. Soon you will reach the final shape.

20. And the even rim is smoothed with a chamois cloth.

21. To make a lip for your pitcher, support the mouth of the pot with one hand, and with the first finger of your other hand pull the clay outward to form a lip.

22. Pull until the lip completes the form you want.

23. The completed pitcher—with handle yet to come.

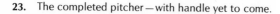

MAKING A LID

1. Lids are usually thrown on the wheel. First measure the diameter of the pot into which your lid must fit. Remember that clay contracts when it is dried and fired.

2. Proceed with the lid by throwing a lump of clay on the wheel and treating it as if you were making a small bowl.

3. Continually measure with a caliper to see if the lid will fit the pot.

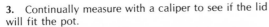

4. If too small, pull the clay outward, forming a small wall.

5. Measure again, with the caliper.

6. Continue pulling out the clay until it is the correct size.

7. Take a trimming tool.

8. With the tool, cut away about a quarter of an inch from the outside.

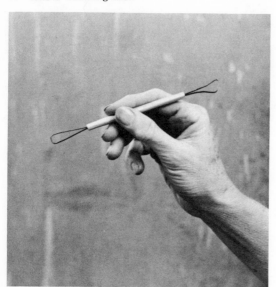

9. This makes an outer rim.

10. At this point, the lid should be a perfect fit for the pot.

11. With wetted fingers, smooth the clay.

12. The finished lid.

TRIMMING THE BOWL

1. Let the pot dry for a day or two, until the clay is leather hard. Then place the bowl upside down on the wheel, packing wet clay around the sides to keep it firm.

2. Start the wheel spinning, and with the sharp point of a trimming tool or knife cut into the outside of the base for about one-half inch.

3. A layer of clay will whip off, leaving a cleanly defined base.

4. Next, cut gently into the base of the pot, from the center outward.

5. Continue this process on about two-thirds to three-quarters of the base area, leaving an outer rim.

6. This process is principally for narrower pieces, not for flat or shallow pots, which only need to be tidied up.

7. A neatly trimmed base.

MAKING A HANDLE

1. Cups and pitchers usually need handles, so this is a process you will use quite often. To begin, take a stiff lump of clay.

2. Keeping your hand wet with plenty of water, pull a handle from this lump.

3. The handle will take on the natural shape of the fingers.

4. Handles can be attached to a piece as soon as it is firm enough to work with — usually an hour or so after throwing.

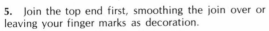

5. Join the top end first, smoothing the join over or leaving your finger marks as decoration.

6. Join the bottom end of the handle.

7. Again, the join can be smoothed over or the finger marks left as part of the pot.

8. The size of the handle should, of course, complement the pot to which it is attached.

9. A view of the finished handle, showing the joins.

OFF THE HUMP

1. Throwing "off the hump" is a good technique for making small objects which should match one another, such as cups. Center a large piece of clay on the wheel.

2. Center a portion of the clay so that a "hump" is created at the top. Now open out the small hump with your thumbs.

3. Draw up the sides of the cup.

4. Using a chamois, even out the sides of the cup.

5. Put the finishing touches on the rim.

6. Refine the interior of the cup with a damp sponge.

7. Remove the cup from the larger piece of clay.

8. Now begin the next cup: center a small portion of the clay remaining on the wheel. Repeat the procedure.

6

Now that your lump of clay has been transformed into the shape and body of a living pot, the time has come to consider what "dress" it can be given. While it is true that unglazed pots — sometimes known as terracotta work — are quite attractive in themselves, you will, in general, want to decorate and glaze your pots to achieve a satisfactory finish.

Bisque firing

First, however, I should explain that the majority of potters, even before decorating their pots, subject them to a first firing in the kiln, known as a bisque firing. This process is described fully in the first part of Chapter 8, but it needs to be emphasized, before considering methods of decoration, that you should first bisque fire your pots.

Among other very good reasons for bisque firing is the simple fact that your pot can be handled much more easily, being now already bone dry and strong. A pot in the raw-clay state can be decorated, but great care would be needed, as it is very easy to knock off a handle or break off a rim. Your bisqued pots can be moved about and turned this way and that with impunity.

No doubt by now you will have made some study of the various forms of pottery decoration used by ancient potters. If not, then make a point of visiting some museums, or at least looking through some good books of pottery reproductions. It is most instructive to see how the potters of Greece and China and Japan have used exquisite designs to decorate their pots. It does not follow that these are necessarily the right effects for contemporary pots, but it will do you no harm to absorb their influence as a basis.

The Appropriate Decoration

One of the first things you should appreciate about the decoration of pottery is that it should be an integral part of the pot itself, of its life and theme. You will find this to be so with most of the early Eastern pots, in particular, but also, if you study them carefully, of many good modern pots as well. If, for instance, you are able to look at some of the pots of Paul Soldner, or of Toshiko Takaezu, or of Rudy Autio or William Wyman, you will find that all their decoration seems to blend into the personality of the pot as a whole. With experience this becomes second nature to a potter. He hardly has to think about what kind of decoration he is going to apply to a certain pot; almost instinctively he chooses the best approach for that particular shape.

Perhaps a simple example may help to illustrate this point. A drawing or painting of a sea view might be very pleasant as such; to try and reproduce it in the same detail on a pot would, obviously, be either impossible or unsuitable. On the other hand a certain pot, partly by its texture,

Thrown pots by Fong Chow (U.S.A.) with blue and green glazes.

might in some way suggest a sea motif. This could be further suggested by decorating it simply with a few lines cut into the glaze, or by a feathering motif. Or possibly it could best be shown by the colors blended in the glazing.

So in your approach to decoration be realistic, be reasonable, and be economic: suggest rather than portray actually. And above all make your decoration a part of the pot, not your pot a part of the decoration.

Slip

Many forms of decoration depend first on your bisque ware being given an over-all coat of slip. This is a mixture of clay and water which is sieved to produce a thin liquid which is poured over the pot (or the pot can be dipped into it in a bucket). The clay must naturally contain some fluxes (Albany slip is one that does), or fluxes, feldspar, and silica must be added in order for the slip to unite with the body upon firing. Slip-clay fluxes are generally the alkaline earth compounds, plus, for color, any of a variety of chemical oxides supplied by manufacturers; these include iron, cobalt, copper, manganese, and so on. Their colors emerge only in the firing; they are not apparent in powder form. You will find that iron oxide gives a color ranging from tan to dark brown, while cobalt added to Albany slip, for instance, gives a beautiful semigloss jet black. The depth of color depends on the thickness with which the oxide is applied. The results can be very beautiful.

Slip Trailing

Once your pot is slipped there are several methods of decoration that can be applied. One, indeed, involves a further use of slip, and is known as *slip trailing*. A slip trailer is simply a syringe (which you can buy at a drugstore). Fill the bulb with one of the colored slips and then squirt out the slip while moving the syringe in some kind of pattern over the pot. For slip trailing at its best, you should apply it to a flat plate or shallow dish, but it can be used effectively on cylindrical pots. There is no limit, of course, to the number of different colors you can use, and interesting results are often obtained by running the slips into one another.

Brushwork

Brushwork is another obvious approach. Using an ordinary paintbrush (but metallic oxides for paints) paint your design onto the slipped pot, bearing in mind that one or two thick brush strokes will probably, in the eventual firing, be more satisfactory than attempts at intricate

Covered stoneware pot by Claude Conover (U.S.A.) with fine incising into which slip was rubbed.

brushwork. Again there is no limit to what you can try with your brush, but from my foregoing remarks I hope you will be as economical as possible.

Banding

Banding is a variation of brushwork. For this you need some form of decorating wheel on which the pot is placed and then turned round. As it moves, you place the tip of the brush against the side and slowly move it up or down — the result will be spiral bands (or if you wish, by removing the brush after each circle, you can get a series of circular bands).

Feathering and Combing

These are two other methods of making impressions on the slip — the first literally by drawing a feather lightly across the surface, the second by literally holding a comb against the side as it is revolved.

Sgraffito

Perhaps the most effective of these kinds of decoration is that known as *sgraffito* designs. Here the pot is first dried off after being slipped, and then a pattern is scratched into it with a special sgraffito tool. A variation of this is what is sometimes called *incising*. Here the pot is taken up before slipping and a pattern or design is cut into it with a sharp tool; later it is glazed over with a transparent glaze so that the incising shows through.

Wax-Resist Decoration

Popular with the commercial potteries is wax-resist decorating. The design is painted on the bisque in wax and then the pot is slipped; the slip will attach itself only to those parts of the pot which are not painted, so that a pattern will be created for the eventual firing.

It is true, in fact, that the large potteries are able to apply a whole range of decorative effects which are, in general, beyond the compass of the home potter. Numerous assistants are employed solely on such processes as gilding, enameling, luster painting, and so on. Printing and lithography are two more of these processes available to the large potteries, but hardly to you.

Nevertheless, you, in turn, can achieve effects which the big potteries might not be bothered about. For instance, you can individually model every pot. You could try giving one a particularly unusual shape or you could take coiled lengths of clay and add them on to a pot to make an embossment. Don't be afraid to experiment in this way; there is always room for imagination. Remember, of course, that the art of decoration is not confined to cylindrical pots—it applies even more importantly to flat slab pots, to ceramic jewelry, and to modeled pots.

SLIP TRAILING

1. Slip trailing is one method of decorating a shallow bowl or platter.

2. A slip trailer is simply a syringe, which you can buy at the drug store, filled with a colored slip.

3. Squirt out the slip while moving the syringe in a pattern over the bowl.

BRUSHWORK

1. For this method of decorating, use an ordinary paintbrush with metallic oxides for paints — and brush your design onto the slipped pot.

2. Economical decoration is most satisfactory here, a few freely done, thick brush strokes.

4. And there is no limit to the number of different colors you can use, with interesting results often obtained by running the oxides into one another.

3. There is no limit to what you can do with the brush.

BANDING

1. Banding is also done with a brush, but for this technique you will need to place your pot on a decorating wheel, so that it can be turned round.

2. As the pot revolves, place the tip of the brush against the side — the result will be a band, or circle.

3. You can decorate your pot with a series of circles, or you can slowly move the brush up and down, giving you a spiral band.

TEXTURES

1. As shown by the following examples, the ways in which you can give texture to your pot are limited only by your imagination.

2. Texture can be the result of additions of clay, or the wet clay can be worked with your finger and/or a sharp tool.

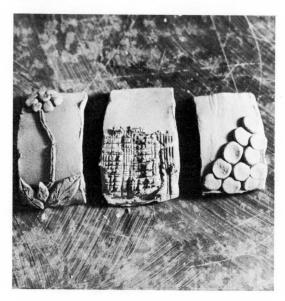

3. Incising is the term for cutting a design into the clay before it is glazed.

4. Texture is best applied to slab and wheel-thrown pots, rather than coiled shapes.

5. Texture can also be given by pressing a stamp into the wet clay.

By Robert Sperry (U.S.A.), covered stoneware bottle with rich surface decoration of painted glazes.

After throwing, the glazing of a pot is the most important single process in pottery making. It is possible to take a lump of clay and fashion it to a beautiful shape; subsequently to apply some decoration and even successfully bisque fire it; but if a pot is incorrectly glazed, or inadequately glazed, then all those efforts are in vain.

The Purpose of Glazing

First, then, let us understand the purpose of glazing. After your pot has been thrown and bisque fired, and decorated if required, it is ready for the chemical process of glazing, or sealing. A glaze is a form of glass which coats the pot—a liquid which hardens at a certain temperature and fuses with the pot, creating a watertight covering. A glaze is made up of alumina, silica, and flux, all substances found in clay; the alumina helps to lower the melting point of the glaze, which would otherwise be too high for a normal pottery kiln. Most studio potters use fritted glazes—that is, glazes which have been mixed with nonsoluble ingredients. A frit is a compound of lead and bisilicate obtained by heating lead and silica together to a high temperature so that they fuse and form a glass; this is then cooled and ground into a fine powder.

Lead glaze
>   4 parts lead bisilicate
>   1 part clay
>   chemical oxide (see section on slips)

Alkaline glaze
>   3 parts borax frit
>   1 part clay
>   chemical oxide

It is better to use alkaline glazes in domestic pottery, made by substituting the alkaline borax frit for lead basilicate.

To make up a glaze you need a bucket, into which the specified quantity of water is poured; then the clay and borax frit are added. These latter will be in the form of powder, probably in lumps. Mix them thoroughly with the water until they form a smooth paste. Then pass the liquid through a 120-mesh sieve, into a second container. Finally wash out the original bucket and resieve the liquid back into the first bucket. Remember to label each bucket with the name of the glaze it now contains, as otherwise you may easily use the wrong one.

By the noted Swedish designer-craftsman Carl-Harry Stalhane, covered stoneware pots with dark green glaze.

Large thrown jar with lid by Otto Heino (U.S.A.).

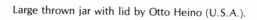

Slab-built and glazed pots by Signe and Klaus Lehmann of Germany.

Stoneware vase combining slab and thrown elements by William Wyman (U.S.A.).

Color Properties of Glazes

Here are a few general hints on the color properties of glazes. When copper oxide is added the effect will be an apple green color; if added to a borax frit glaze, the color will be nearer to turquoise. Particularly striking results can be obtained by adding copper.

Manganese gives a violet and dark reddish hue if added to borax and a brown color if added to a lead glaze. Iron oxide will give a tan color; cobalt produces black or blue, preferably toned down by the addition of copper or manganese. More brilliant colors can be achieved by adding borax, soda ash, pearl ash, sodium bicarbonate, and potassium dichromate to the glaze.

White Opaque Glaze

If you wish to produce a white opaque glaze, then mix tin oxide with a transparent glaze — from five to seven percent Zircopax will also turn glazes opaque, but it is not as effective as tin.

Black Luster Glaze

Manganese can be mixed with cobalt to produce a black luster; on its own, up to five percent per solid weight, it will produce colors in the brown range. Chromium produces green at a high temperature. Antimony will give yellow.

You will find, of course, that there are all kinds of possibilities with the mixing of oxides into glazes. It is well worth having a special glazing notebook in which you record the results of these experimental mixtures. Naturally, if you were making pottery fired at much higher temperatures, such as stoneware, then you would obtain quite a different set of results. But, at least in your beginnings as a potter, you would be wiser to master earthenware glazing first.

While experimentation with making glazes of your own is a good way of learning more about pottery making, it might be more convenient for you to purchase your glazes in prepared form. This is simply done (you will find a list of manufacturers at the end of this book). The glazes are purchased in powder form and simply need to be mixed with water to the specified amount. At least this way you are less likely to make any disastrous mistakes! But don't let it preclude later experimentation. Later on, for example, the ash formed from burning wood of various kinds, grass, etc., can be used for variations.

So much for glazes and their properties, from a functional point of view. You should remember, as well, that glazes can be used as the only form of decoration. Here again it is a case of finding out by (sometimes bitter) experience. The trouble with relying on glazes for decoration is that very often you will find it impossible to repeat an effect exactly — so be wary of this.

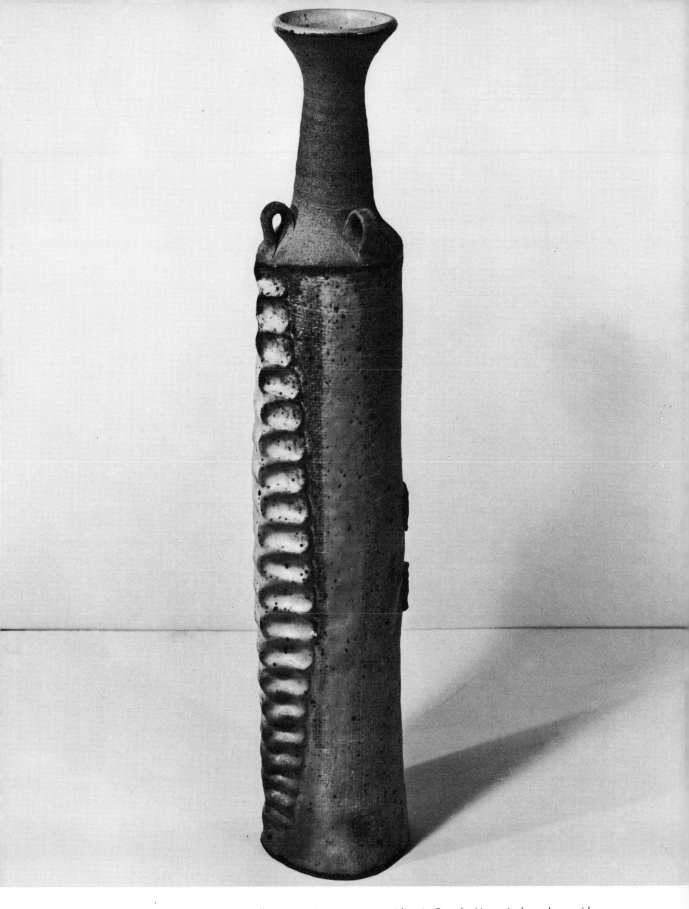

Bottle by Dean Mullavey, a U.S. potter now residing in Canada. Note pinch marks on side.

Procedure

Now we come to the act of glazing the pot. Generally, your glaze will be in a bucket or some such container. In fact the glazing is done very much as the slipping. Pick up the pot to be glazed, take a jug of glaze and pour it inside and swill around, then empty back into the bucket. This has glazed the inside of your pot. Now, in order to glaze the outside, hold the pot by its foot and immerse up to the level of the base (try if possible not to get glaze onto the actual base; if this should happen, be sure to sponge it off afterward).

An alternative method is to stand your pot (this would apply in particular to large pots) on two wooden dowel rods above the bucket, and actually pour the glaze all over the pot, and also inside. Some studio potters now also use the spraying technique, and you may like to do this. Any ordinary spray would do. In fact, you can apply glaze even with a brush, but obviously this is a more laborious method than dipping or spraying. In general, brushing is used to apply a band or a decorative panel of glaze. Also remember that you can decorate your pots by over-glazing—that is, after firing one glaze at a high temperature, you then paint on another glaze which fires at a much lower temperature, obtaining a double glaze effect. Sometimes the application of a transparent glaze over an opaque one can give an appealing result.

Never be in too much of a hurry to end the glazing process; there is always something you may have forgotten. For instance, at all costs don't forget to take a sponge and examine each pot meticulously after it has been glazed, to make sure the base is clear of glaze. This is most important, for if your glazed pot is put in the kiln with glaze on the bottom it will probably stick to the shelf of the kiln during the firing, thus ruining both pot and shelf (an expensive item). Also check that no pieces of glaze have been knocked off; if necessary, retouch with a brush.

GLAZING

1. To make your glaze, add clay and borax frit (see text) to a specified quantity of water, mixing until a smooth paste is formed.

2. Pour the liquid through a 120-mesh sieve into another container.

3. Pour your glaze into a pitcher, then take your pot and pour the glaze into it.

4. Swill the glaze around the inside of the pot, to cover it completely, and pour the liquid out.

5. There are several methods for glazing the outside of a pot. One way is to hold it by the foot and pour glaze over it.

6. Be sure to hold the pot over the glaze container so that the excess will not be wasted.

7. Using the same procedure, you can glaze the interior of a pot. Note that you can eradicate previous decorations with some glazes.

8. You can combine one method of decorating for the exterior and another method for the interior.

8

If throwing a pot can be regarded as the act of creation, then perhaps it is fair to call the firing process the act of fulfillment. Despite the many processes which you may have applied to your pot—wedging the clay, throwing the ball, trimming, handling, slipping, decorating, glazing—all this work will be wasted if at the end there is a bad firing. For each pot is the sum total of the clay and its properties, the thrower and his capabilities, the art of decoration and of glazing, and finally the success of the firing. It is in the firing that the clay and its slip and glaze and decorations are brought to fusion point to achieve the final effect of a finished pot.

Firing Temperature

Let us then first be sure we understand the processes of firing. Most potters fire their pots twice. That is, first they subject the raw pots to a medium or *bisque firing* (usually to a temperature of about 1475° F.-1650° F.), and afterwards they refire the glazed pots to a much higher temperature (about 2000° F. if earthenware, above 2300° F. if stoneware, and even higher for certain specialized forms of pottery such as porcelain).

The firing of pottery is carried out today in modern kilns, made of special firebrick capable of withstanding tremendous heat. At large commercial potteries these kilns may be huge, may even in fact consist of several kilns linked by a tunnel system. Most studio potters find the most convenient form of kiln heating to be electricity, and you would probably be well advised to follow their example. Electricity is convenient, easily accessible, reasonably cheap, and simple to operate. Firing an electric kiln can literally be as simple as turning a switch.

The Kiln

Before using an electric kiln, perhaps we should make quite sure that its operation is clearly understood. The minimum size recommended would be a kiln for temperatures to 2000° F., with a firing chamber (i.e. the actual firing area of the kiln) of about eighteen inches by eighteen inches by fifteen inches. Along the inner walls of this kiln, and possibly along the floor area, too, there will be electrical elements, which are connected at the rear and led by means of one master cable to the electricity supply. At the side of the kiln, or possibly on the wall close by it, will be the operating switch to bring the kiln's circuit into operation. Kiln firing times vary with the size of the inner chamber and the amount of pots contained, but, approximately speaking, a kiln of the size suggested would take about six hours to reach a temperature of 1650° F., and perhaps eight hours to reach 2000° F. After that you would need to allow approximately the same period of time before opening the kiln doors.

Accessories

In order to use an electrical kiln properly you need a certain number of accessory products: *shelf supports,* ceramic pieces which slot into each other to provide a support for shelves; *stilts,* tiny ceramic tripods used for standing pots on — and, of course, flat lengths of fire clay which are laid upon the props to make successive *shelves* on which to stand pots. You will also need some method of determining the inner temperature of the kiln — either a *pyrometer,* a fairly expensive piece of electric equipment which the maker will supply ready fitted, or (more commonly used) a set of *pyrometric cones,* which are fingers of glaze materials tested to melt at specific temperatures. To use the cone, simply place it in line with the peep hole of the kiln so that by looking in every now and then you can judge when the cone has melted down.

Bisque Firing

Now to the two firing processes: first *bisque firing.* The inconvenience of this is that the pots are still raw and therefore easily broken, whereas for a glaze firing they are firm and most unlikely to break; on the other hand a convenience of bisque firing is that no shelves are needed and that, provided care is used, the pots can be packed side by side, touching, and even one on top of another. This enables a great number of pots to be loaded into one bisque firing — probably two or three times as many as would be accommodated in a glaze firing.

When your pots are all loaded, shut the kiln doors, smear some clay round the edges if there are any bad fits, and check, by looking through the peep hole, to make sure that the cone can be clearly seen. Now switch on the kiln. Some potters believe in switching the kiln on and off to make the heating process safely slow, but in fact this is seldom necessary. Simply leave the kiln on now for several hours, and then after five hours or so begin checking to see if the cone has melted. As soon as it has melted, switch off the kiln and allow it to cool for approximately the same number of hours. Finally open the kiln and remove the now bisqued pots for the next stage of decoration and glazing.

Glaze Firing

For the second *glaze firing,* a great deal more care will be needed. First, you must remember that no glazed pots can be allowed to touch; furthermore, even after insuring that the bases are un-glazed it is also a wise precaution to mount each pot on a stilt. All this means that in loading your kiln you have to build layer by layer, a process which in itself requires some planning; for

Cast and thrown stoneware by Ettore Sottsass, Jr., of Italy, painted with matte and glossy glazes.

Covered stoneware storage jars by U.S. potter Kenneth Ferguson, wheel-thrown and glazed.

instance, it is best to start with two or three levels of fairly shallow pots, such as bowls, leaving taller pots to the top shelf. Finally, don't forget that this time you will need a different cone, one that will melt at 2000° (instead of about 1650° for the bisque firing).

Otherwise the operation follows the lines of bisque firing. Switch on the kiln and go away and do some other work until it is time to keep an eye on the kiln for melting. Finally switch it off and allow the kiln to cool.

When at last the kiln is sufficiently cooled open the doors carefully — no matter how cool the interior may have become, the rush of outside air will probably cause a bit of commotion among the pots, and it is probably wise then to half close the doors again for another ten minutes or so before attempting to unload the kiln.

Defects in Firing

Possibly your first kiln firing will be a modest one, perhaps even just a handful of pots, but I am sure you will find it a very exciting experience. Don't be surprised, however, if the results are hardly what you expected. They seldom are at first. Until you become practiced at loading glaze kilns, for instance, you may easily find that you have allowed two pots to stand touching, so that the glazing has joined them. Alternatively, you may not have cleaned the bottoms well enough and the glaze has run down and stuck the pot to the shelving. As I say, don't be disheartened, this happens to the best intentioned of beginning potters (and to quite a few more experienced ones). If a mishap occurs, you should immediately try to analyze the error so that you will not repeat it.

There are a few other possible troubles that may be encountered. One of the most common is *blistering* — that is, parts of the glaze tend to bubble. Sometimes, too, glaze will be found to be *jumping* off the pot in thin lengths — often you will find that this is the result of taking the pot out of the kiln too soon. A variation of this trouble is *crawling*, a glaze defect generally caused by an excessive application of glaze which cracks upon drying. In the firing these cracks do not fuse but tend to separate further, exposing the clay body. Finally one might mention *crazing*, the appearance in the finished pot of a network of tiny cracks. This is usually due to underfiring, but is not necessarily serious; many potters actually strive to obtain this effect. The cure is to fire higher.

After every firing of your kiln you should automatically make a record of the number of pots fired and the result of the firing — this is a great help to you both as a record and a guide for future firings.

It is difficult to think of any further problems likely to be encountered in firing kilns. They are essentially simple "machines" which, like the kitchen oven, operate efficiently year after year with very rare exceptions. All that can go wrong with your kiln, in fact, is that at some stage you may burn out one or more of your elements. The sort of kiln you will be using will probably have six or eight elements of a fairly common kind, and these can be replaced at any time. Otherwise depreciation is very small, for the firebricks should endure for many, many years, though, if necessary, a particular brick can be replaced fairly easily.

Wood-fired porcelain bottles by Ruth McKinley (U.S.A.), glazed in pale greens, pinks, grays, and creams, the tallest 12" high.

Flower jars by Byron Temple (U.S.A.), the lower sections left unglazed, the upper parts painted in blues and grays.

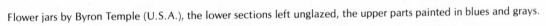

Wheel-thrown stoneware bottle by Japanese potter Hiroaki Morino with ash glaze and comb tracing.

Once you have learned the craft of pottery, in all probability in a class or workshop situation, it can only be a matter of time before you will want to practice ceramics in your own home. The point about setting up a home pottery is that it involves a fair initial outlay, but after that the expenditure is very modest — whereas there are many other hobbies, such as painting or photography, where, over a long period, the expenditure would probably be even higher.

In the second half of this chapter you will find some approximate costs, from which you can see that the outlay involved covers quite a wide range, depending on whether you wish to buy all equipment new or second hand, and whether you are prepared to try making your own wheel or kiln. Fortunately there are only two really expensive items in the equipment of a pottery, the wheel and the kiln, and thanks to the present widespread interest in ceramics there are now many firms which supply these items at reasonable costs.

Studio

First things first, however. You need a room of your own — the bigger the better, though size is not a vital factor (I know a well-established professional potter who still has his studio in a basement ten feet by six feet). Here, obviously, everything is going to depend on circumstances. If you live in a one room apartment, then it would be infeasible to set up a pottery in such limited quarters, and you would have to consider renting a room or basement nearby. But otherwise, if you live in a house with a spare room, or a basement — or alternatively a house with a garden large enough to accommodate a wooden or corrugated iron shed — then, with a little ingenuity, you should be able to secure adequate premises for your pottery.

Whatever the size and shape of your room, you must bear in mind that it needs good lighting, a supply of electric power, and access to water. Running water is an advantage in any pottery, but failing that you can always manage with a large jug and a bowl.

Now that we have our pottery room, let's think about equipping it. It is best to devote some thought to the general layout, according to the space available. Whether small or large a pottery needs to be very much a functional place. It is no use, for instance, storing the clay next to the kiln, for it would go hard and be useless. Nor is there much point in setting up the wheel and kiln together, for there are many processes that take place between the throwing and the firing. Bear in mind that the "chronological" processes of pottery making are: storing clay, preparing clay, throwing, storing thrown pots, handling, trimming, lipping, slipping, decorating, glazing, loading the kiln and firing, and storing the finished pots.

Clay

Taking these requirements in this order, the first and most obvious item is the basic material, *clay*. For the home potter I would strongly advise making use of the service provided by manufacturers who specialize in preparing clay ready for use. (A list of names and addresses will be found at the end of the book.) For your purposes you would need a red or a gray prepared clay, earthenware, firing at about 1950°F. Local supplies of earthenware clays are available in many parts of the country. Since they are widely used in cement, plaster, and mortar mixtures, they are competitively priced and generally quite reasonable.

Storage Space

Next you will need to consider a means of storing your clay—preferably not in the studio, where there is too much heat, but in a cupboard or some other cool place. When you decide to use the clay you will need a wedging table. A good strong *kitchen table* is excellent, and you can usually pick one up on sale for a few dollars. If necessary cover the surface with formica or plywood.

Your wedging table will, of course, serve other purposes. It can be used for rolling out lumps of clay, as a surface for resting molds or slabs, as a place for pots in various stages.

Shelving

This brings us to the important matter of *shelving*; in my experience you can never have too much, but of course there are space considerations. One very simple procedure is to fit a series of six-inch brackets up the side of the wall and to have a stack of flat boards (about three feet long by six inches wide) which can be put on the brackets when and as required. Some of your shelving, of course, will need to be permanent, and here it is often quite satisfactory to make use of old cupboards, bookshelves, and similar items. The purposes of the shelving, it might be added, are for storing pots, bottles, glazes and oxides, tools, technical books, and so on.

Potter's Wheel

Now we come to the *potter's wheel*. The kind of wheel installed is entirely a matter of choice and finance, and the cheapest possible kind of wheel would be a homemade kick wheel. Most readers may feel, at least at this stage, that they would prefer to buy a ready-made wheel, and personally I think this is a good idea. Building your own wheel and kiln is the kind of specialized

Pottery by Joulia of France combining thrown and slab elements.

Small raku pot by Paul Soldner (U.S.A.).

Unglazed stoneware bottle hand-built by Karen Werner (U.S.A.) with inlaid coils in center section, 21″ high.

activity which is better embarked on from a position of experience and knowledge, after several years in pottery. What sort of wheel would you prefer — a kick wheel or a powered wheel? There are a few aesthetic arguments for the former, and certainly a kick wheel is the cheapest type. Several firms supply a reliable kick wheel, and their names and addresses are listed at the end of this book. Prices may differ according to type and size, but you should get a good new kick wheel for $175 to $185. Taking a different approach, you can buy a second hand kick wheel and save probably half that amount. If you decide to do this then the obvious thing is to advertise in magazines such as *Craft Horizons* or *Ceramic Monthly* or, possibly, in your local newspaper. Whether you get a new or a good secondhand wheel, the operational principle is so simple and straightforward that there is no reason why it should not serve you for many years without trouble.

More and more modern potters, however, are turning to the use of electric wheels, and you may prefer to do the same. At one time the price was rather prohibitive for a home potter, but in recent years the increased demand has enabled firms to cut down prices to a more reasonable level. The kind of electric wheel suitable for you as a home potter is usually supplied in a compact form with a ten-inch wheel head, operated by a one-fourth horsepower 110 volt (AC) motor, with variable speeds from 80 to 200 rpm. Several firms make electric wheels (some with foot pedal control of the gears, others with switch control) at prices from $320 up; you will find them listed at the end of this book.

Small Tools

Next, going round our imaginary studio in order of use, we come to the various small tools and accessories which will be required, both for preparing and throwing the clay, and for later processes. First, you will need a length of *copper wire* for cutting off pieces of clay — also, for use while throwing, a *sponge*, a wooden *trimming tool*, a piece of *chamois leather*, a *needle* (for cutting off tops of pots). After the throwing is over comes the decorating, and for this work you have a choice of a *sgraffito tool, modeling tools, paintbrushes*, according to the type of decoration you have in mind. When it comes to making slips or mixing glazes, you will need a close-meshed (120) *sieve* plus, of course, at least half a dozen household *buckets*, always useful for mixing glazes and slips. As a last note on the subject of accessories, don't forget such useful objects as *bowls, pitchers*, and *bins*; or such administrative items as *books* in which to record kiln firings and glaze recipes.

Chemical oxides — cobalt, copper, manganese, etc. — which are the principal media for decoration, can be obtained in a wide variety from any of the manufacturers listed at the end of the book. *Glazes* can also be obtained ready-made from the manufacturers, though most potters prefer, with experience, to evolve their own glazes, by a process of trial and error. *Lead bisilicate* is a basic part of most glazes and can if necessary be obtained from your local drugstore; but for a home potter much the simplest procedure would seem to be to write to one or two of the big dealers, such as Jack D. Wolfe or Rovin Ceramics, who will supply vast catalogs listing everything you could conceivably need, from oxides and glazes to wheels and even kilns.

Kiln

This brings us to the last major item in our list of equipment—the *kiln*. As was indicated in the earlier chapter on firing, electrically operated kilns are most generally used, and these would seem the most practical for a home pottery, where space, convenience, and cleanliness are probably important. Some of the industrial firms' kilns are almost as big as small houses, but of course what you need is something quite the reverse—a compact, well insulated kiln with a firing area of about eighteen inches by eighteen inches by fifteen inches. You can get a very small kiln for firing ceramic jewelry that is only about six inches deep, and you may, in view of costs, prefer to start with one of these smaller ones. However, taking a longer view, I would recommend, if possible, aiming at a medium sized kiln of approximately the measurements I have suggested. You will find a list of firms at the end of this book, and prices would range from $155 upwards.

Pyrometric Cones

Pyrometric cones can be bought in lots by the hundred, so they are very economical. There is a cone for every temperature up to 2600° F. However, if you have extra money to spare you can get the manufacturer to fit a pyrometer in your kiln, and this gives you an immediate reading of the temperature on an outside gauge.

10

In this chapter I am going to suppose that the reader, though having, I hope, enjoyed and profited from the preceding chapters, now feels the need of some practical instruction in ceramics. There may be many readers who know little or nothing about craft study opportunities in the United States, so it may help to give a few general details.

Wherever you live, you will be very unlucky if you are not within reach of museum schools or arts and crafts centers, both of which usually offer courses in ceramics. For those who work during the day there are evening classes, but for those able to do a full-time course there are day classes, of course.

Among the subjects covered in such courses would be construction methods, throwing, decorating, glazing, etc., and there might be visits to local potteries, museums, and other such centers. There would, of course, be practical instruction by trained potters, experienced in all the various processes. Over a period you would learn to throw pots, and selected pots would be decorated, glazed, and fired.

The following is a selective list of such schools in various parts of the country. Unless noted, courses in ceramics are offered during summer sessions as well as during the regular school year.

Arkansas
School of Art and Drama, Arkansas Arts Center, Mac Arthur Park, Little Rock.

California
Cultural Arts Division of the Los Angeles City Department of Parks and Recreation, Los Angeles.
Richmond Art Center, Civic Center Plaza, 25th and Barrett, Richmond.

Delaware
Delaware Art Center, 2301 Kentmere Parkway, Wilmington.

Florida
Art League of Manatee County School, 209 Ninth Street West, Bradenton.

Georgia
Columbus Museum of Arts and Crafts, 1251 Wynnton Road, Columbus.

Iowa
Des Moines Art Center, Greenwood Park, Des Moines.

Kansas
School of Wichita Art Association, 401 North Belmont, Wichita.

Massachusetts
Boston YWCA Workshops, 140 Clarendon Street, Boston. No summer courses in pottery.
Plymouth Pottery Guild, 42 Summer Street, Plymouth. In summer, only special students are occasionally accepted for short, concentrated periods of study. Regular workshops during the rest of the year, however.
Craft Center, 25 Sagamore Road, Worcester.

Minnesota
Saint Paul Art Center, 30 East Tenth Street, Saint Paul.

New Jersey
The Museum School of the Montclair Art Museum, 3 South Mountain Avenue, Montclair. No summer session.

New York
Adult Program of the Great Neck Public Schools, 345 Lakeville Road, Great Neck, Long Island.
Brooklyn Museum Art School, Eastern Parkway, Brooklyn.
Clay Art Center, 40 Beech Street, Port Chester. Operates primarily as a workshop for potters working independently, but classes for beginners and advanced students are given three times weekly.
Craft Students League, West Side Branch YWCA of the

City of New York, 840 Eighth Avenue, New York.

Greenwich House Pottery, 16 Jones Street, New York. Summer classes for advanced students only.

Westchester Workshop, County Center, White Plains.

Oregon

Museum Art School of the Portland Art Museum, Southwest Park at Madison, Portland.

Workshops of Art of the Salem Art Association, 600 Mission Street, Salem.

Tennessee

Craft Workshop in the Smokies, Pi Beta Phi Settlement School, The University of Tennessee, Gatlinburg.

Texas

Museum School of Art, 1001 Bissonet, Houston.

Virginia

Virginia Museum of Fine Arts, Robinson House Leisure Class Program, Boulevard and Grove Avenue, Richmond.

West Virginia

Oglebay Institute Center, 841-1/2 National Road, Wheeling.

If you are really serious about becoming a professional potter, there are many colleges and universities throughout the country which allow you to major in ceramics, or include a range of ceramics courses in the art department curriculum. The list of such institutions that follows also includes a few places of special instruction for the professionally-oriented potter, such as Pond Farm Potteries in California, where the well-known ceramist Marguerite Wildenhain teaches all aspects of the craft to a limited number of students.

Arizona

Arizona State College, Flagstaff.

California

California College of Arts and Crafts, Broadway at College Avenue, Oakland.

California Institute of the Arts, 743 South Grand View Street, Los Angeles.

California State College, Long Beach.

Humboldt State College, Arcata.

Mendocino Art Center, Little Lake Street, P.O. Box 36, Mendocino.

Pond Farm Pottery, Guerneville.

Sacramento State College, 6000 Jay Street, Sacramento.

San Francisco Art Institute, 800 Chestnut Street, San Francisco.

San Jose State College, San Jose.

Scripps College, Claremont.

University of California, Berkeley.

University of California at Los Angeles.

University of the Pacific, Stockton.

Colorado

Adams State College, Alamosa.

Colorado State College, Greeley.

Colorado State University, Fort Collins.

University of Denver, School of Art, Denver.

Connecticut

Silvermine College of Art, New Canaan.

District of Columbia

Catholic University of America, Washington.

Corcoran School of Art, New York Avenue and 17th Street, Northwest, Washington.

Florida

University of Tampa, 401 West Kennedy Boulevard, Tampa.

Georgia

Georgia Southern College, P.O. Box 2032, Statesboro.

Georgia State College, 33 Gilmer Street, Atlanta.

Illinois

Augustana College, Rock Island.

Bradley University, Peoria.

Rockford College, Rockford.

Rosary College, River Forest.

Southern Illinois University, Carbondale.

University of Illinois, Champaign.

Indiana
Herron School of Art, 100 East 16th Street, Indianapolis.
Indiana University, Bloomington.
Purdue University, Lafayette.

Iowa
Clarke College, Dubuque.
Cornell College, Mount Vernon.
University of Iowa, Iowa City.

Kansas
University of Kansas, Department of Design, Lawrence, Kansas.

Kentucky
Murray State College, Murray.
Ursuline College, 3105 Lexington Road, Louisville.

Louisiana
Newcomb College, Department of Art, Tulane University, New Orleans.

Massachusetts
Massachusetts College of Art, Ceramic Department, Brookline and Longwood Avenues, Boston.
School of The Museum of Fine Arts, 230 The Fenway, Boston.
University of Massachusetts, Amherst.

Michigan
Albion College, Albion.
University of Michigan, Ann Arbor.

Minnesota
Concordia College, Moorhead.
School of the Associated Arts, 344 Summitt Avenue, Saint Paul.
University of Minnesota, Deluth.

Mississippi
The University of Mississippi, Columbia.

Missouri
Northwest Missouri State College, Maryville.
Southeast Missouri State College, Cape Girardeau.
Southwest Missouri State College, 901 South National, Springfield.
Stephens College, Columbia.
University of Missouri, Columbia.

Montana
Montana State University, Missoula.

Nebraska
Doane College, Crete.
University of Nebraska, Lincoln.

New Hampshire
University of New Hampshire, Durham.

New Mexico
New Mexico Highlands University, Las Vegas.

New York
School for American Craftsmen of the Rochester Institute of Technology, 65 Plymouth Avenue South, Rochester.
Skidmore College, Saratoga Springs.
State University College at New Paltz, New Paltz.
State University of New York College of Ceramics at Alfred University, Alfred.
Teachers College, Columbia University, 525 West 120th Street, New York.

Ohio
Cleveland Institute of Art, 11141 East Boulevard, Cleveland.
Lake Erie College, Painesville.
Ohio University, Department of Industrial Arts, Athens.
Wittenberg University, Springfield.

North Carolina
East Carolina College, Box 2704, Greenville.

Oklahoma
University of Oklahoma, Norman.
The University of Tulsa, 600 South College, Tulsa.

Oregon
Oregon College of Education, Monmouth.
Oregon State University, Corvallis.

Pennsylvania
Allegaheny College, Meadville.
Pennsylvania State University, University Park.
Tyler School of Art of Temple University, Beech and Penrose Avenues, Philadelphia.

Tennessee
East Tennessee State University, Johnson City.

George Peabody College for Teachers, Nashville.
The Memphis Academy of Arts, Overton Park, Memphis.

Texas
Hardin Simmons University, Abilene.
North Texas State University, Denton.
Texas Christian University, Fort Worth.
Texas College of Arts and Industries, Kingsville.
Texas Western College of the University of Texas, El Paso.

Utah
University of Utah (Department of Art, Building 441), Salt Lake City.

Virginia
Longwood College, Farmville.

Hampton Institute, Hampton.
Richmond Professional Institute, 901 West Franklin Street, Richmond.

West Virginia
West Virginia University, Creative Arts Center, Morgantown.

Wisconsin
Mount Mary College, 2900 North Menominee River Parkway, Milwaukee.
University of Wisconsin, Department of Art and Art Education, 219 Education Building, Madison.
University of Wisconsin—Milwaukee, 3203 North Downer Avenue, Milwaukee.
Wisconsin State University, Platteville.
Wisconsin State University, Whitewater.

Training in ceramics need not be limited to museum schools, arts and crafts centers, or the universities and colleges. You should make full use of other available educational programs. For instance, in various parts of the country there are summer schools which offer short-term, concentrated courses in ceramics, usually augmenting instruction in materials and techniques with a varied schedule of lectures, seminars, and demonstrations. While some of these programs are directed primarily to the student with some knowledge of his craft, most welcome the beginner. Although it would naturally be impossible to learn pottery making in a two- or three-week session, some useful basic information should be gained.

All summer schools included in the listing below offer beginning courses in ceramics, with the exception of the two specified.

BROOKFIELD CRAFT CENTER, Brookfield, Connecticut.
FLETCHER FARM CRAFT SCHOOL, Ludlow, Vermont (winter address, Chelsea, Vermont).
JOHN C. CAMPBELL FOLK SCHOOL, Brasstown, North Carolina.
HAYSTACK MOUNTAIN SCHOOL OF CRAFTS, Deer

Isle, Maine. For advanced craftsmen only.
PENLAND SCHOOL OF CRAFTS, Penland, North Carolina. Two-and three-week sessions for intermediate and advanced students.
WILLIMANTIC SUMMER ART AND CRAFT WORKSHOP, Willimantic State College, Willimantic, Connecticut.

What is a good pot? How does one appreciate pottery? The longer you pursue the art and craft of pottery the more general knowledge you will gain, but it does not necessarily follow that you will be able to answer these questions, though many people seem to have an instinct about them. Certainly I would advise letting your instinct have its say. If you see a pot and feel that you want to pick it up, that in itself is a good sign. The pot has made an impact on you; it must have some quality.

Here are a few questions you might ask yourself:

Is this pot a whole pot?
Has the shape integrity?
Does the shape fulfill the intention?
Is the decoration suitable to the pot?
If there is a handle is it well and truly made?
Are the lines of the pot in harmony?

And so on. There are many other questions that could be asked, and which you may think about. The more you sit and look at a pot the more questions will come to your mind, and in answering them you are in fact learning to appreciate this particular pot, and therefore the art of ceramics as a whole.

In *A Potter's Book*, Bernard Leach outlined some of the points which he would apply to judging a pot. He emphasized, for instance, the importance of the ends of lines — lines are forces and the points at which they change or cross are especially significant. He suggested that vertical lines are of growth, power, and yearning; horizontal lines are of rest, of earth and the even flow of life; and diagonal lines are of change. Curves make for beauty and angles for strength; a small foot gives grace, a broad one stability. He went on to suggest that the straight line and curve, the square and the circle, the cube and the sphere are the potter's polarities, which he works with a rhythm of form under one clear concept.*

Above all, when trying to appreciate a pot, try to understand what may have been in the potter's mind. For instance, don't allow some apparent blemish to produce a conditioned reaction. A blemish in a pot, paradoxically, can be part of its charm. The whole point about pottery, and therefore about any single pot, is that it is an expression of individuality: the pot is the potter. In pottery, as in some other crafts, technique is by no means everything. There must be added to the technique something of the personality of the creator, something which is almost impossible to define.

---

*These are age old symbols, simple enough to be useful in design, beautiful in themselves, and yet having a definite significance.

There are, of course, many different kinds of pots, and everyone will have private preferences. A very large number of people would readily appreciate the beautiful colorings of some of the ancient Korean and Chinese pots. On the other hand you may be conditioned more to appreciate contemporary trends.

One of the best ways of learning to appreciate pots, of course, is to visit museums and exhibitions, as I have mentioned in the previous chapter. Here you have the opportunity to see side by side examples of some of the world's greatest pots. It is well worth spending an afternoon browsing among such exhibits as Grecian vases, Korean pots, Egyptian urns, Roman tablets, Italian faience and majolica; pay attention to the characteristics of each, and then try to see if you can discover their influences on modern pots. With practice you will soon develop an eye for certain points. For instance, you will quickly learn to tell a thrown pot from a molded pot. Paradoxical as it might seem at first to you, the most perfectly and uniformly shaped pot is almost certain to be the molded one.

Many people become so interested in studying the history of pottery, so immersed in technical data of the Greek and Byzantine ages, that they deviate from practicing the craft itself. I hope you will resist this temptation. Besides, there is nothing that will help you to understand good pottery quite so much as continual participation yourself. When you are continually going through the same processes as other potters through the ages it is inevitable that you acquire their way of approaching all the problems of pottery. And once you acquire this approach, then I think you will find you are really understanding pottery.

Above all, try and approach pottery as an essentially physical craft. You do not feel the pages of a book or even the canvas on which a picture is painted; but instinctively you feel the pot. There is a famous Chinese pot which was inscribed with the message *For the Imperial Fondling of Ch'ien Lung*. This epitomises very well this aspect of the pot—the desire to touch and make contact.

Like sculpture, pottery is three-dimensional and should be seen as such. There are many similarities between sculpture and pottery, and it is not surprising that many potters enter the field of sculpture and vice versa.

In conclusion, and bearing in mind the vast field covered by pottery—which after all includes such diverse forms as earthenware, stoneware, porcelain, china, and terra cotta—always approach the understanding of pots and pottery in a spirit of true humility. If you wish to put yourself in the right mood, just stand in front of some ancient pot and reflect that perhaps two thousand years ago a fellow mortal stood at a wheel and fashioned from a lump of clay this living thing. That, in essence, is the ageless marvel of pottery.

12

Pottery has a long history of its own; it is one of the most ancient of all crafts and has proved of great benefit to archaeologists in the tracing of old civilizations. Flesh and blood are quickly destroyed, but pots live on forever!

As you become more proficient at pottery you will almost certainly want to know more about its history. A visit to The Metropolitan Museum of Art in New York alone will surely stimulate your interest; its great collections cover five thousand years of world history. but in particular you will want to see the Nathan Cummings collection of pre-Columbian art, the John D. Rockefeller, Jr., collection of Chinese porcelains, and the R. Thornton Wilson collection of European ceramics.

There are, of course, many other museums and institutions across the country which have notable collections of old ceramics. Among them is the Art Institute of Chicago, whose Oriental department, spanning the arts of China from the pre-Han through the early Ch'ing dynasties, is rich in ceramics. Also at the Institute are notable groups of English pottery, including the Frank W. Gunsaulus collection of Wedgwood and the Amelia Blanxius collection of English pottery and porcelain.

At the Wadsworth Atheneum in Hartford, Connecticut, you can see Italian majolica, French and Meissen porcelain, the latter being among the finest in existence. Not too far away, at New Haven, Connecticut, is the Yale University Art Gallery with the Stoddard collection of Greek and Roman vases. Important collections of Chinese and Japanese ceramics are owned by the Cleveland Museum of Art and the M. H. de Young Memorial Museum in San Francisco, which also boasts an outstanding collection of Persian pottery. For historical ceramics of North America, one of the best sources is The Henry Francis du Pont Winterthur Museum, five miles outside of Wilmington, Delaware, whose collection of American decorative arts from 1640 to 1840 is considered the finest and largest collection of its kind ever gathered. Actually, even your smaller local museum may well have an excellent collection—in Phoenix, for instance, at the Heard Museum there is a fine group of prehistoric and historical crafts of all primitive peoples, especially Southwestern Indian cultures. So make full use of local museums to get the atmosphere of ancient pottery.

Collections of contemporary ceramics are much more limited and can usually best be seen in circulating exhibitions at the country's major museums, including the Museum of Contemporary Crafts in New York and Museum West in San Francisco. The Everson Museum of Art in Syracuse, New York, however, is well known for a notable collection of contemporary American ceramics based on prize winners from past Ceramic National exhibitions.

To get you started, here is a listing of some museums in the United States, including the ones already mentioned, which have sizable groups of pottery in their collections.

Large hand-built planters by Louis Krevolin and Elizabeth Constantine (U.S.A.).

Bottle and pot in tooled stoneware by British craftsman Lucie Rie.

Alabama
Montgomery Museum of Fine Arts, Montgomery.

Arizona
Heard Museum, Phoenix.

California
E. B. Crocker Art Gallery, Sacramento.
Fine Arts Gallery of San Diego, Balboa Park, San Diego.
Long Beach Museum of Art, Long Beach.
Los Angeles County Museum, Los Angeles.
M. H. de Young Memorial Museum, San Francisco.

Connecticut
Slater Memorial Museum, New London.
Wadsworth Atheneum, Hartford.
Yale University Art Gallery, New Haven.

Delaware
The Henry Francis du Pont Winterthur Museum, Wilmington.

District of Columbia
Freer Gallery of Art, Smithsonian Institution, Washington.
Institute of Contemporary Arts, The Meridian House, Washington.
National Gallery of Art, Washington.

Hawaii
Honolulu Academy of Arts, Honolulu.

Illinois
Art Institute of Chicago, Chicago.
Illinois State Museum of Natural History and Art, Springfield.

Indiana
South Bend Art Center, South Bend.
University of Notre Dame Art Gallery, Notre Dame.

Kansas
Wichita Art Museum, Wichita.

Kentucky
J. B. Speed Art Museum, Louisville.

Louisiana
Isaac Delgado Museum of Art, New Orleans.

Louisiana State Museum, New Orleans.

Maine
Bowdoin College Museum of Art, Brunswick.
Colby College Art Museum, Waterville.

Maryland
Walters Art Gallery, Baltimore.

Massachusetts
Harvard University, William Hayes Fogg Art Museum, Cambridge.
Museum of Fine Arts, Boston.
Museum of Fine Arts, Springfield.
Old Sturbridge Village, Sturbridge.
Williams College Museum of Art, Williamstown.
Worcester Art Museum, Worcester.

Michigan
Cranbrook Academy of Art Galleries, Bloomfield Hills.
Detroit Institute of Arts, Detroit.

Minnesota
Minneapolis Institute of the Fine Arts, Minneapolis.
Walker Art Center, Minneapolis.

Missouri
City Art Museum of St. Louis, St. Louis.
William Rockhill Nelson Gallery of Art, Kansas City.

Mississippi
Springfield Art Museum, Springfield.

New Jersey
Newark Museum, Newark.
Princeton University, The Art Museum, Princeton.

New Mexico
Museum of New Mexico, Fine Arts Building and Museum of International Folk Art, Santa Fe.

New York
Albany Institute of History and Art, Albany.
Brooklyn Museum, Brooklyn.
Cooper Union for the Advancement of Science and Art, Museum for the Arts of Decoration, New York.
Everson Museum of Art, Syracuse.
Memorial Art Gallery, Rochester.
Metropolitan Museum of Art, New York.

Museum of the American Indian, New York.

Ohio
Cincinnati Art Museum, Cincinnati.
Cleveland Museum of Art, Cleveland.
Ohio Wesleyan University, Department of Fine Art, Delaware.
Toledo Museum of Art, Toledo.

Oklahoma
Philbrick Art Center, Tulsa.

Oregon
Portland Art Museum, Portland.

Pennsylvania
Museum of Art, Carnegie Institute, Pittsburgh.
Philadelphia Museum of Art, Philadelphia.

Texas
Museum of Fine Art of Houston, Houston.

Virginia
Virginia Museum of Fine Arts, Richmond.
Colonial Williamsburg, Williamsburg.

Washington
University of Washington, Henry Art Gallery, Seattle.

Like any other craftsman, the potter has — and needs — the advantages of a number of organizations set up to serve his special requirements. When you have become moderately proficient at ceramics, you might wish to join one or other of these organizations.

The largest of these (approximately 25,000 members) is the American Craftsmen's Council which has its headquarters in New York, an office and museum in San Francisco, and regional representatives throughout the country. The aim of the Council is a very practical one: to act as a center for exploring professional problems — marketing procedures, contacts for commissioned work, opportunities for study, places to exhibit — with individual craftsmen, and to provide a source of advice and information for interested laymen throughout the country. To this extent the Council might be considered only of general interest to the potter, but the fact is that ceramics is one of the most active crafts in the United States, and many studio potters have received assistance and inspiration from the Council's program of conferences, exhibitions, and lectures — as well as its handsome magazine *Craft Horizons*. At the time of this writing, there is a Contributing Member category at a yearly fee of $25, an Annual Supporting Member classification ($15), a Craftsman Member level ($10) and a Subscribing Member category ($8). All memberships receive the magazine, and there are increasing benefits at each level. For further information, write directly to the Council at 44 West 53rd Street, New York, New York.

Of more specific interest might be local ceramics organizations, such as the Association of San Francisco Potters, the Michigan Potters Association, etc. These groups are formed to promote, stimulate, ensure, and protect the future of craftsmen producing high quality work and to this end organize regular meetings, sponsor exhibitions, and exchange technical information.

Apart from the American Craftsmen's Council and the local potters' associations, there are a great many thriving general craft organizations to which potters belong. In addition, in almost every area you will probably find at least one art society which would be only too happy to add a craftsman to its members.

A list of general craft and pottery organizations follows:

American Ceramic Society, Design Division, 464 North Kilkea Drive, Los Angeles, California.

Arizona Designer-Craftsmen, Box 4036, Tucson, Arizona.

Artist-Craftsmen of New York, c/o R. Leigh Glover, 45 East 85th Street, New York, New York.

The Arts and Crafts Association, 610 Coliseum Drive, Winston-Salem, North Carolina.

Association of San Francisco Potters, 255 Monticello Street, San Francisco, California.

Bainbridge Arts and Crafts, Inc., Box 161, Bainbridge, Washington.

Bay Area Arts and Crafts Guild, 180 Bella-Vista Drive, Hillsborough, California.

Carmel Crafts Guild, P.O. Box 4333, Carmel, California.

Ceramic Club, c/o Peter Craft, Rhode Island School of Design, Ceramic Department, Providence, Rhode Island.

Ceramic Guild of Bethesda, c/o Lucy Collins, 4212 Oakridge Lane, Chevy Chase, Maryland.

Ceramic League of Miami, c/o Mrs. R. C. Benitez, 901

University Drive, Coral Gables, Florida.

Clay Club, c/o Carol Youngberg, 6200 111th Avenue N.E., Kirkland, Washington.

Colorado Artist Craftsmen, c/o Mrs. Donald Daily, 704 14th Street, Boulder, Colorado.

Colorado Potters Guild, c/o Miss M. D. Johnson, 50 East Louisiana Avenue, Denver, Colorado.

Community Arts and Crafts, c/o Mrs. Gerry Letaw, 584 Remington Drive, Sunnyvale, California.

Craft Foundation of Woodstock, c/o Mr. John McClellan, Woodstock, New York.

The Craft Guild of Dallas, c/o Mr. Paul Harris, 3521B Dickason Avenue, Dallas, Texas.

Creative Crafts Council, 8904 Fairview Road, Silver Spring, Maryland.

Designer-Craftsmen of California, c/o Ida Dean Grae, 424 La Verne, Mill Valley, California.

Designer-Craftsmen of Rhode Island, 53 Transit Street, Providence, Rhode Island.

Florida Craftsmen, c/o P. C. Holler, Route 6, Box 120, Jacksonville, Florida.

Georgia Designer-Craftsmen, c/o Robert Westervelt, Agnes Scott College, Decatur, Georgia.

The Inlet Potters Club, c/o Miss Opal VanKommer, 4613 Spenard Road, Spenard, Alaska.

The Kiln Club of Washington, D.C., c/o Pauline Eis, 2709 Spencer Road, Chevy Chase, Maryland.

League of New Hampshire Arts and Crafts, 205 North Main Street, Concord, New Hampshire.

Lexington Arts and Crafts Society, 130 Waltham Street, Lexington, Massachusetts.

New Orleans Crafts Council, 7823 Oak Street, New Orleans, Louisiana.

Maine Coast Craftsmen, The Old Spalding House, South Thomaston, Maine.

Mansfield Fine Arts Guild, Inc., c/o Mrs. John Kindel, 40 South Park Street, Mansfield, Ohio.

Massachusetts Association of Craftsmen, 71 Newbury Street, Boston, Massachusetts.

Michigan Potters Association, c/o Eugene Riemann, 4746 Second Avenue, Detroit, Michigan.

Midwest Designer-Craftsmen, c/o Florence Resnikoff, 7321 South Constance, Chicago, Illinois.

New Mexico Designer-Craftsmen, c/o Lee Weber, Montezuma, New Mexico.

Northwestern Michigan Artists and Craftsmen, c/o Sally Long, 7568 Pennsylvania Drive, Traverse City, Michigan.

Parkersburg Clay Club, 922 Julian Street, Parkersburg, West Virginia.

Pennsylvania Guild of Craftsmen, 1320 Ketchner Road, Bethlehem, Pennsylvania.

Pennsylvania Guild of Craftsmen — Bucks County Chapter, c/o O. Willner, R.D. 1, New Hope, Pennsylvania.

Plymouth Pottery Guild, 42 Summer Street, Plymouth, Massachusetts.

The Portland Potters Group, 7400 S.W. Ridgemont Street, Portland, Oregon.

Potters Guild of Baltimore, P.O. Box 4827, Baltimore, Maryland.

Richmond Craftsmen's Guild, 4003 Patterson Avenue, Richmond, Virginia.

The Society of Arts and Crafts, 71 Newbury Street, Boston, Massachusetts.

Society of Connecticut Craftsmen, c/o Mrs. L. Gratiot, 88 Water Street, Stonington, Connecticut.

Texas Designer-Craftsmen, c/o C. J. Suckle, Art Department, Southwest Texas State College, San Marcos, Texas.

Toledo Potters Guild, 3528 Worden Road, Oregon, Ohio.

Tulsa Designer-Craftsmen, c/o Mrs. J. Patrick Manha, 221 East 29th Street, Tulsa, Oklahoma.

Woodstock Guild of Craftsmen, Inc., Woodstock, New York.

York State Craftsmen, c/o Dorothy Byer, The Cornell Public Library, 417 West State Street, Ithaca, New York.

Stoneware "lazy susans" by Karen Karnes (U.S.A.) combining thrown forms.

Planter by Waltrud Wiemers and Doris Yokelson (U.S.A.), made by throwing seven bowl shapes and attaching them to the tall centerpiece, also thrown.

14

CLAYS

California
L. H. Butcher Co., 15th and Vermont Streets, San Francisco.
Cannon and Co., Box 802, Sacramento.
Garden City Clay Co., Redwood City.
Gladding, McBean and Co., Lincoln.
S. Paul Ward, Inc., 60 Mission Street, South Pasadena.
Western Ceramic Supply Co., 1601 Howard Street, San Francisco.
Westwood Ceramic Supply Co., 610 Venice Blvd., Venice.

Colorado
Denver Fire Clay Co., 3033 Black Street, Denver.
Van Howe Co., 1185 South Cherokee Avenue, Denver.

Illinois
Illinois Clay Products Co., Barber Building, Joliet.
Western Stoneware Co., Monmouth.

Indiana
American Art Clay Co., Inc., Indianapolis.

Louisiana
La Mo Refractory Supply Co., 323 Iris Avenue, New Orleans.

Maine
Rowantree Pottery, Blue Hill.

Maryland
Pottery Arts Supply Co., 2554 Greenmount Ave., Baltimore.

Massachusetts
Newton Pottery Supply Co., Newton.

Michigan
General Refractories Co., 7640 Chicago Avenue, Detroit.
Rovin Ceramics and Pottery, 7456 Fenton Street, Dearborn.

Missouri
Christy Firebrick Co., 506 Oliver Street, St. Louis.

New York
Stewart Clay Co., Inc., 133 Mulberry Street, New York.
Jack D. Wolfe Co., Inc., 724 Meeker Avenue, Brooklyn, New York.

New Jersey
Mandl Ceramic Supply Co., 35 Fogerty Drive, Trenton.
United Clay Mines Corporation, Trenton.

Ohio
Cedar Heights Clay Co., 50 Portsmouth Road, Oak Hill.
Croxall Chemical and Supply Co., P.O. Box 757, East Liverpool.
Kentucky-Tennessee Clay Co., Mayfield.
Zanesville Stoneware Co., Zanesville.

Pennsylvania
Ketcham Architectural Tile Co., 125 North 18th Street, Philadelphia.
Langley Ceramic Studio, 413 South 24th Street, Philadelphia.
Roder Ceramic Studio, 500 Broadway, Clifton Heights.

Texas
Trinity Ceramic Supply Co., 9016 Diplomacy Row, Dallas.

WHEELS

J. T. Abernathy, Ceramic Studio, 212 South State Street, Ann Arbor, Michigan.
Advanced Kiln Co., 2543 Whittier Boulevard, Los Angeles, California.
A. D. Alpine, Inc., 11837 Teale Street, Culver City, California.
American Art Clay Co., 4717 West 16th Street, Indianapolis.
Craftools, Inc., 401 Broadway, New York, New York.
H. B. Klopfenstein and Sons, Route 2, Crestline, Ohio.
Harvey Littleton, Route 1, Verona, Wisconsin.
Randall Wheel, Box 531, Alfred, New York.
Skutt and Son, Box 202, Olympia, Washington.
Paul Soldner, Aspen, Colorado.

TOOLS

American Art Clay Co., 4717 West 16th Street, Indianapolis.
L. H. Butcher Co., 15th and Vermont Streets, San Francisco.
Craftools, inc., 401 Broadway, New York, New York.

B. F. Drakenfeld, Inc., 45 Park Place, New York, New York.

O. Hommel Co., 209 Fourth Avenue, Pittsburgh, Pennsylvania.

Roder Ceramic Studio, 500 Broadway, Clifton Heights, Pennsylvania.

Tepping Ceramic Supply Co., 3517 Riverside Drive, Dayton, Ohio.

Van Howe Co., 1185 South Cherokee Avenue, Denver, Colorado.

S. Paul Ward, Inc., 60 Mission Street, South Pasadena, California.

Westwood Ceramic Supply Co., 610 Venice Boulevard, Venice, California.

KILNS

J. T. Abernathy, 212 South State Street, Ann Arbor, Michigan.

Allied Engineering Corp., 4150 East 56th Street, Cleveland, Ohio.

A. D. Alpine, Inc., 11837 Teale Street, Culver City, California.

American Art Clay Co., 4717 West 16th Street, Indianapolis, Indiana.

Denver Fire Clay Co., 3033 Black Street, Denver, Colorado.

Dickinson Kilns, Inc., 2424 Glover Place, Los Angeles, California.

W. H. Fairchild, 712 Centre Street, Freeland, Pennsylvania.

L. and L. Manufacturing Co., Chester, Pennsylvania.

Paragon Industries, Inc., Box 10133, Dallas, Texas.

Roder Ceramic Studio, 500 Broadway, Clifton Heights, New Jersey.

Unique Kilns, 530 Spruce Street, Trenton, New Jersey.

CERAMIC CHEMICALS

L. H. Butcher Co., 15th and Vermont Streets, San Francisco, California.

Ceramic Color and Chemical Manufacturing Co., P.O. Box 81, New Brighton, Pennsylvania.

Croxhall Chemical and Supply Co., P.O. Box 757, East Liverpool, Ohio.

George Fetzer, 1205 17th Avenue, Columbus, Ohio.

Gare Ceramic Supply Co., 165 Rosemont Street, Haverhill, Massachusetts.

Illini Ceramic Service, 163 West Illinois Street, Chicago, Illinois.

Kraft Chemical Co., 917 West 18th Street, Chicago, Illinois.

Langley Ceramic Studio, 413 South 24th Street, Philadelphia, Pennsylvania.

Newton Pottery Supply Co., Newton, Massachusetts.

Trinity Ceramic Supply Co., 9016 Diplomacy Row, Dallas, Colorado.

Vitro Manufacturing Co., 60 Greenway Drive, Pittsburgh, Pennsylvania.

Paul S. Ward, Inc., 60 Mission Street, Pasadena, California.

Western Ceramic Supply Co., 1601 Howard Street, San Francisco, California.

Westwood Ceramic Supply Co., 610 Venice Boulevard, Venice, California.

Whittaker, Clarke and Daniels, Inc., 260 West Broadway, New York, New York.

Jack D. Wolfe Co., Inc., 724 Meeker Avenue, Brooklyn, New York.

Wheel-thrown porcelain bottle by Rosa Cabat (U.S.A.) with gray, blue, and green glazes, 9″ high.

Thrown bottle by U.S. potter Karen Karnes.

Books about pottery run into the hundreds, and books on the history of the craft continue to appear almost as frequently as contemporary studies on the craft and technique. Your local librarian will no doubt be pleased to advise you on a selected list. In the meantime, here are some recommended titles — books on process and philosophy as well as historical surveys.

A POTTER'S BOOK by Bernard Leach, Transatlantic Arts, Inc., Hollywood-by-the Sea, Florida, 7th American edition 1956, 294 pages. $7.50.

CENTERING in Pottery, Poetry and the Person by Mary Caroline Richards, Wesleyan University Press, Middletown, Connecticut, 1964, 159 pages. $8.

CERAMICS by Glenn C. Nelson, Holt, Rinehart and Winston, Inc., New York, New York, 1960, 236 pages. $5.95.

CERAMICS FOR THE ARTIST POTTER by F. H. Norton, Addison-Wesley Publishing Co., Inc., Reading, Massachusetts, 1956, 320 pages. $7.50.

CERAMIC SCULPTURE by Ruth H. Randall, Watson-Guptill Publications, Inc., New York, New York, 1948, 95 pages

CLAY AND GLAZES FOR THE POTTER by Daniel Rhodes, Chilton Co., Scranton, Pennsylvania, 1957, 219 pages. $7.50.

GREEK PAINTED POTTERY by R. M. Cook, Quadrangle Books, Inc., Chicago, Illinois, 1962, 391 pages. $12.50.

HAND-BUILT POTTERY by Josephine R. Krum, International Textbook Co., Scranton, Pennsylvania, 1960, 116 pages. $6.50.

HOW TO MAKE POTTERY AND CERAMIC SCULPTURE by Julia Hamlin Duncan with Victor D'Amico, (Museum of Modern Art) Simon and Schuster, New York, New York, 1947, 95 pages. $2.50

IRANIAN CERAMICS by Charles K. Wilkinson, (Asia House Gallery Publication) Harry N. Abrams, Inc., New York, New York, 1963, 145 pages. $8.50.

PAPAGO INDIAN POTTERY by Bernard L. Fontana and others, University of Washington Press, Seattle, Washington, 1963, 163 pages. $5.75.

POTTERY: FORM AND EXPRESSION by Marguerite Wildenhain, (American Craftsmen's Council) Reinhold Publishing Corp., New York, New York, 1959, 149 pages. $6.50.

STONEWARE AND PORCELAIN by Daniel Rhodes, Chilton Co., Philadelphia, Pennsylvania, 1959, 217 pages. $7.50.

THE CERAMIC ART OF JAPAN by Hugo Munsterberg, Charles E. Tuttle Co., Rutland, Vermont, 1964, 272 pages. $12.50.

THE COMPLETE BOOK OF POTTERY MAKING by John B. Kenny, (Greenberg) Chilton Co., Philadelphia, Pennsylvania, 1949, 242 pages. $7.50.

THE POTTER'S CRAFT by Charles Binns, Van Nostrand New York, New York, 3rd edition 1947, $4.00.

THE TECHNIQUES OF PAINTED ATTIC POTTERY by Joseph V. Noble, Watson-Guptill Publications, 1965, 260 pages, $17.50.

THE WARES OF THE MING DYNASTY by R. L. Hobson, Charles E. Tuttle Co., Rutland, Vermont, 2nd edition 1962, 234 pages. $12.50.

Magazines and Periodicals

As magazines devoted exclusively to ceramics in the U.S.A. are few and oriented either to industry or the hobby potter, far and away the most highly recommended publication to readers of this book is one which covers all craft fields, *Craft Horizons*. Published six times a year by the American Craftsmen's Council, it usually contains articles on American and foreign ceramics and has a continuing series of professional-level workshop articles, many of which focus on various aspects of the ceramic medium. Beautifully illustrated and well edited, it is obtained by becoming a member of the American Craftsmen's Council (44 West 53rd Street, New York, New York, and the lowest annual fee is $8.

Other magazines and professional journals are:

CERAMIC AGE, 9 Chester Building, Cleveland, Ohio. An industrial magazine.

CERAMIC MONTHLY, 3494 North High Street, Columbus, Ohio. For the hobbyist, although containing many articles useful to the beginning potter.

JOURNAL OF THE AMERICAN CERAMIC SOCIETY, Columbus, Ohio. Technical articles of little interest to readers of this book.

You also might be interested in a magazine from England entitled POTTERY (Pendley Manor, Tring, Herts, England). Edited by a practicing potter, this magazine takes a more philosophical approach to the field than the American publications.

Vase by Jeff Schlanger (U.S.A.) in heavily grogged clay with impressed stamp design.

Covered jar in glazed and tooled stoneware by U.S. potter Marguerite Wildenhain, 11″ high.

Banding. Form of glaze or slip decoration made by holding brush tip against moving pot.

Blistering. Bubbles appearing on pot after glaze firing.

Blow Outs. Explosion of clay during firing due to the presence of impurities.

Bone China. Hard translucent chinaware produced chiefly in England. The body contains a large amount of bone ash.

Borax Frit. Compound of borax and silica used for making glazes.

Carving. Method of decorating by cutting a pattern on clay surface.

Casting. Method of producing molded pots from plaster molds.

Centering. First stage in making a pot on the wheel.

China. Pottery made from mixture of kaolin, feldspar, ball clay, and flint.

Coiling. Making pots from rolls of clay which are coiled round and round.

Collaring. Method of narrowing neck of a pot by squeezing with fingers.

Combing. Decorating by drawing a comb across wet/or glaze slip.

Crawling. A glaze defect generally caused by an excessive application of glaze, which cracks upon drying.

Crazing. Minute cracking of glaze, usually caused through underfiring.

Decorating Wheel. Small turntable on which pots can be revolved.

Earthenware. Type of pottery fired at around 2000 F.

Feldspar. Mineral material from which clay derives.

Fettling. Process of tidying bottoms of pots after glazing.

Finishing Tool. Sharp pointed tool used for tidying and trimming pots.

Firing. Term used to describe baking pots in a kiln.

Flux. A constituent of a glaze, used to lower melting point.

Frit. Compound of silica and lead, borax, etc.

Glaze. Coating applied to a pot to render it waterproof.

Grog. Powdered hard fired clay, used for strengthening ordinary clay when making large articles.

Impressing. Method of decorating by pressing object into clay surface.

Incision. Scratching decorations onto unfired clay.

Kaolin. Pure clay, also known as china clay.

Kiln. Furnace made of refractory clay in which pots are fired.

Kneading. Method of removing air from clay.

Majolica. Tin-glazed type of earthenware pottery, sometimes known as faience, originating from Italy.

Molds. Plaster pieces from which shapes of clay are molded.

Oxides. Metallic chemicals used for coloring slips and glazes.

Pinchware. Name given to pots made by pinching clay to desired shape.

Porcelain. Type of pottery, like china, firing from $2300°$ to $2670°$F.

Pulling a Lip. Forming lip of pot by pulling out with fingers.

Pyrometer. An instrument, fitted into kiln, for measuring temperatures.

Pyrometric Cones. Cones of glaze material designed to melt when specific temperatures are reached in a kiln.

Raku. Type of earthenware covered with lead glaze and fired at low temperature.

Raw Clay. Clay which has not yet been fired.

Reduction. Method of cutting down oxygen in kiln and affecting glazes.

Refractory. Term used to describe types of clay which withstand high temperatures.

Running. Effect of overfiring, causing glazes to run off pot on to floor.

Sgraffito. Type of decoration made by scratching through slip or glaze.

Silica. Constituent of sand and glazes, used in making glazes.

Sillimanite. A material used in making kiln shelves, highly refractory.

Slip. Clay in liquid suspension.

Slip Trailing. Decoration by trailing slip over pot's surface, using a syringe.

Stoneware. Pottery which fires at higher temperature than earthenware, above $2300°$F.

Terra Cotta. An earthenware body, generally red in color and containing grog.

Throwing. Term used to describe making a pot on a wheel.

Trimming. Method of hollowing out foot or lid of a pot.

Vitrification. Description of what happens when particles of clay fuse.

Wax Resist. Method of decorating by applying melted wax and slipping or glazing.

Wedging. Method of removing air from clay.

By Gertrud and Otto Natzler (U.S.A.), bottle with green-blue crystalline glaze, bowl with "mariposa" reduction glaze.

Thrown pot by Vivika Heino (U.S.A.) with brushed slip and glaze decoration.

Edited by Hal Halverstadt
Designed by Wm. Harris
Demonstration Photographs by Louis Mervar
Pottery Demonstrations by Deborah Uscott and Jane Hartsook at the
Greenwich House Pottery, New York City
Photocomposition in ten point Optima by Noera-Rayns Studio, Inc.
Printed by Halliday Lithograph Corporation
Bound by The Haddon Craftsmen, Inc.